10 WOMEN WHO HELPED SHAPE AMERICA

Short Plays for the Classroom

Edited by Sarah Glasscock

SCHOLASTIC
PROFESSIONAL BOOKS

New York • Toronto • London • Auckland • Sydney

Acknowledgments

The editor wishes to thank the talented and resourceful playwrights who contributed to this book. As always, this project couldn't have been completed without the help and support of writer Mary Pat Champeau, who always meets deadlines, and editor Virginia Dooley, who keeps me on track.

Cover design by Vincent Ceci and Jaime Lucero
Cover illustration and interior illustrations by Mona Mark
Interior design by Frank Maiocco

ISBN: 0-590-89645-8

Table of Contents

Introduction

This collection highlights the lives of only ten American women, but there are many, many more who have contributed in significant ways to our country. We hope these plays will launch your students into an exploration of women's roles in history.

This book centers on women who were born before the Civil War. The collection begins with the story of **Francisca Hinestrosa**, a Spanish woman who disguised herself as a man and accompanied De Soto's expedition to Florida. As yet, no biography of her has been written, and historians over the years have been unable to agree on her role. Many of your students may know that **Elizabeth Blackwell** was the first woman doctor in America, but they may not know that she was partially blind. **Ida B. Wells-Barnett** continued to write and speak out against racial injustice even after her newspaper office was burned to the ground. **Queen Liliuokalani**, Hawaii's last reigning monarch, fought for a new constitution that would return power to the Hawaiian people.

A common thread runs through these women's lives: they were all determined to reach certain goals. They worked long and hard. Risking society's disapproval—and often, their lives—these women succeeded. Through their sacrifices, our lives today have been made better. We owe these and other groundbreaking women our thanks. Women have always been a force in our history. We are just beginning to tell all their stories.

Description of Plays and Teaching Guides

The focus of this collection is to broaden students' awareness of women's roles in American history. Feel free to tailor the presentation of these plays to your classroom; some students may enjoy acting and producing the plays, while others may feel more comfortable simply reading aloud their parts in a readers' theater presentation. The important thing is that *all* students participate in the plays. Rotate roles so that everyone gets the opportunity to appear in a play. Boys may protest that the plays are about women, and that the girls in the class will always have the best roles. Obviously gender is an important aspect of this collection, but it shouldn't matter in the casting of the plays. Encourage girls to take on male roles and boys to tackle women's roles. Playing characters very different from themselves may help deepen students' perceptions about the people and times portrayed in the plays.

Each play is followed by a teaching guide. This section begins with a quote by or about the woman or a fact about her or her times. A biography follows which provides further information about the woman's life. You may share it with students either before or after they present the play. *Take a Closer Look* is a bibliography containing, in most cases, biographies of the woman and other books that shed light on the time in which she lived. Set out these books and others that you feel are appropriate for students to study before they read the plays. The teaching guide ends with activities designed to strengthen students' oral, writing, and researching skills. Whenever possible, encourage students to work cooperatively on these activities and to share their work with the rest of the class.

Once you've performed some of the plays, you might ask your class to come up with their own top ten list of American women that they admire. Each student should list her or his choices in order; number one would be the American woman they most admire. Let the class compile their lists into one master list. Invite students to work with a partner, or in small groups to research one or more of the women they have listed. They may use their data to make a classroom display which includes photographs or drawings of the women and details about their lives.

You may want to add the following books to your resource shelf:

Herstory: Women Who Changed the World edited by Ruth Ashby and Deborah Gore Ohrn (Viking, 1995)
Founding Mothers: Women of America in the Revolutionary Era Linda Grant DePauw (Houghton Mifflin, 1975)
American Women: Their Lives in Their Words edited by Doreen Rappaport (Harper Trophy, 1992)

When and How to Put on the Plays

These ten plays have been designed to enrich your existing curriculum and may be used in conjunction with your social studies curriculum. The readers' theater format will also bolster your language arts program; reading the plays aloud will build students' oral literacy and reading skills. The plays will also fit well into thematic units.

As you go through the school year and your students become familiar with the format of the plays, you may find that they want to put on more elaborate productions involving props, scenery, and costumes. They may even want to tinker with the content of the plays themselves! Those students who resist performing will find that there are many behind the scenes roles they can fill. Increase, or add, crowd scenes so students can be on-stage without having to undertake speaking roles.

Regardless of how you and your students decide to produce these plays, be sure to encourage them to make these plays their own.

Francisca Hinestrosa

Exploring America
By Sarah Glasscock

Characters (in order of appearance)

Narrator
Francisca Hinestrosa: Spanish explorer
Hernando Bautista: Francisca's husband, a soldier (referred to as Bautista)
Hernando De Soto: Spanish explorer
Cabeza de Vaca: Spanish explorer
Dona Isabel: De Soto's wife
Juan Ortiz: Spanish man stranded in Florida
Luis de Mosco: Captain of De Soto's Florida expedition
Spanish soldiers 1-2 (nonspeaking roles)
Chief Tuscaloosa: Leader of the Muskhogeans
Muskhogeans 1-4 (nonspeaking roles)
Gregorio: Spanish soldier

ACT 1

Scene 1: 1538. Seville, Spain. At a party in the home of Hernando and Dona Isabel De Soto.

Narrator: After exploring Nicaragua and Peru, Hernando De Soto returned to his home in Seville, Spain, as a rich and famous man. Another famous explorer, Cabeza de Vaca, often visited the De Soto home. No one listened to the two explorers' stories more intently than Francisca Hinestrosa.

Francisca Hinestrosa: Just imagine! Being shipwrecked and wandering in a strange land for eight years!

Bautista: Cabeza de Vaca doesn't look as if he'd been lost for eight years. Living with the Indians and eating nuts and cactus must agree with him.

Francisca Hinestrosa: Let's go speak to him. I have a million questions to ask him.

Bautista (whispering): Wait! Did I tell you that King Charles himself had to ask De Soto for a loan? It's true! The kingdom was about to run out of gold! De Soto saved the day!

Francisca Hinestrosa: And after everything he's done already—fighting so hard in Peru to claim the land for Spain. De Soto deserves all the riches he brought back.

Bautista: Dona Isabel doesn't look too happy about Cabeza de Vaca being here.

Francisca Hinestrosa: She waited such a long time for De Soto to return to Spain. She missed him. I think she missed him almost as much as I would miss you if you ever went away. (sighing) But I understand, too, why De Soto listens to Cabeza de Vaca's stories with such excitement. Think of it! Exploring new territory, seeing things you've never seen before—

Bautista (laughing): Don't sign up for De Soto's expedition without me!

Francisca Hinestrosa: Of course not. I would miss you too much.

(They approach De Soto, Dona Isabel, and Cabeza de Vaca.)

Hernando De Soto: Cities of gold, you say?

Cabeza de Vaca: Yes, yes! Every group of Indians I met said that there were cities and palaces deeper inside the country. The people have so much silver and gold that they don't know what to do with it all.

Dona Isabel: But you didn't see any gold or silver yourself, did you? Or any signs of such great cities?

Hernando De Soto: Even if the stories of gold and silver are greatly exaggerated, the land in the New World is still valuable. It can support farmers. Spain needs to settle this Florida territory as soon as possible, or else France or Portugal will claim it.

Dona Isabel: I agree. And there are many fine Spaniards who could lead such an expedition to Florida. (turning to Francisca and her husband) Ah! Francisca and Bautista, so good to see you. You've met Cabeza de Vaca, haven't you?

Cabeza de Vaca (bowing): My pleasure.

Francisca Hinestrosa: I have so many questions to ask you! What were the people like? How cold were the winters? What about the summers? Were they—

Bautista and Dona Isabel: Francisca!

Hernando De Soto (laughing): Francisca, I believe you'd be the first one to sign up for an expedition to Florida! What about you, Bautista? Could I convince you to come along with me?

Francisca Hinestrosa: Not without me!

Scene 2: A few months later.

Narrator: Just a few months later, King Charles chose Hernando De Soto to lead an expedition to explore and claim the Florida territory for Spain. Dona Isabel would travel with the expedition as far as Cuba, where she would take over her husband's title and duties as Governor of Cuba. Bautista jumped at the chance to join De Soto's expedition—and so did Francisca. With the help of her husband, she disguised herself as a man and went to sign up.

Hernando De Soto: I knew I could count on you to join me, Bautista! Who's this with you?

Bautista (nervously): This is my cousin. He's—he's come to Seville to see if you'll let him join the expedition.

Francisca Hinestrosa (speaking in a deep voice): It's a pleasure, sir. I look forward to the challenge.

Hernando De Soto: Tell me about yourself. What skills do you have? What experience do you have in sailing and soldiering?

Francisca Hinestrosa: I haven't had much experience, sir, in either. But I'm willing to work hard.

Hernando De Soto (thoughtfully): You seem very . . . young, and not very strong. It won't be an easy journey. The country in Florida's very rough. It's filled with swamps. We'll be wading through coral reefs. Bautista, you must knock the dreams of gold and glory out of your young cousin's head.

Bautista: Sir, I've never met anybody in my entire life who's more determined than my wi—my cousin here.

Francisca Hinestrosa: I promise, sir, I won't disappoint you.

Hernando De Soto: Very well then. Pack your things. We leave in a week's time.

(Francisca and Bautista move off.)

Francisca Hinestrosa (in her normal voice): It worked! It worked!

Bautista: Welcome to the expedition—cousin!

ACT 2

Scene 1: 1540. Outside the village of Ocita in what is now Florida.

Narrator: The expedition set sail. After two months, they landed in Cuba. De Soto drilled his soldiers and sent scouts to Florida. Dressed like all the other soldiers, Francisca worked hard. No one suspected that she was a woman! In another two months, on May 18, the expedition left Cuba. The ships landed 12 days later off the coast of Florida. De Soto claimed the land for Spain.

The expedition marched deeper into the Florida territory. Other Spanish explorers had been this far before. They'd treated the native people badly, making them suspicious of the new arrivals. One of the men from an earlier expedition, Juan Ortiz, was discovered living with a group of Native Americans. He joined De Soto and served as translator. The expedition soon made another discovery.

Bautista: What if we hadn't come along when we did? Juan Ortiz would be stuck here forever! It could happen to us, too. We could be stranded here—lost forever.

Francisca Hinestrosa (in her normal voice): There are a thousand of us. How can a thousand soldiers get lost?

Bautista: We shouldn't have wandered so far away from camp. That's how people get stranded. No one knows where we are.

Francisca Hinestrosa: But just look at that tree! Have you ever seen such a tree? Look how the moss hangs from its branches!

(Luis de Mosco steps into the clearing where Francisca and Bautista are standing.)

Luis de Mosco: I thought I was going crazy! No, I said to myself. No, Luis, you cannot be hearing the voice of a Spanish woman! There are no Spanish women within a hundred miles of here!

Bautista: It was a parrot, sir! I heard it myself and almost fell over!

Francisca Hinestrosa (in a deep voice): It's true, sir.

Luis de Mosco: Oh, no, you don't. It's too late now. I recognize you, Francisca Hinestrosa! Come on now! Let's see what De Soto has to say about this!

Scene 2: A few minutes later. In the village of Ocita.

Juan Ortiz: The Indians don't trust you, De Soto. You can give them all the gifts you have and promise that you and your men want to be their friends, but they won't believe you. The Spaniards who came here before you treated them very badly.

Hernando De Soto: Chief Mococco has treated you well and protected you. I will make him understand that some men are good, and some are bad. I've claimed this territory for Spain. I don't want any trouble with the people here, but I will fight them if I have to. I want this land safe for Spanish settlers.

Luis de Mosco (hurrying up to De Soto): Excuse me, sir, a problem has arisen.

Hernando De Soto: What is it?

Luis de Mosco: You won't believe it, sir, until you see for yourself.

Hernando De Soto (impatiently): Show me then.

Luis de Mosco: Bring them over!

(Two Spanish soldiers escort Francisca and Bautista to De Soto.)

Hernando De Soto: Bautista and his cousin—well, what have they done?

Luis de Mosco: Take a closer look, sir.

Francisca Hinestrosa (in her normal voice): It was my idea entirely. My husband—

Bautista: No, no, sir, this is all my fault. I didn't want to leave her in Spain. I knew I would miss her too much.

(Hernando De Soto surprises everyone by beginning to laugh.)

Hernando De Soto: Francisca Hinestrosa! Dressed up as a soldier! You certainly had us fooled! Good job, good job!

Bautista: You're not angry with us?

Francisca Hinestrosa: You won't send me back to Cuba, will you? I've turned into a good soldier—

Hernando De Soto: I'm sorry to say that your soldiering days are over, Francisca. You can stay on, but you're now the expedition's cook and nurse.

Francisca Hinestrosa: But sir, I'm a good soldier. I've worked hard. I don't know anything about being a nurse, and my cooking is—

Bautista: I must say, sir, her cooking is pretty awful.

Hernando De Soto: Soldiers do not disobey orders. You learned to be a good soldier, Francisca. Now, I expect you to be a good cook and a good nurse.

Francisca Hinestrosa: I will, sir, I promise. But if you should ever need another good soldier, I can do that, too.

ACT 3

Scene 1: October, 1540. In what is now Alabama.

Narrator: The expedition marched north, further into Florida. They fought several battles with the native people. Francisca Hinestrosa helped treat the wounded soldiers. Moving into what is now Georgia, the expedition had an easier time. There, they met many Indian leaders, including Cofita, head of a large Creek Village. She gave De Soto baskets filled with pearls. Then the expedition turned southwest toward present-day Alabama and the lands of Chief Tuscaloosa. The expedition expected trouble.

Chief Tuscaloosa: I greet you as a brother, De Soto. Lodgings have been prepared for you.

Hernando De Soto: I didn't want to leave these lands without meeting you. I would be happy if we became friends. I invite you to ride with me on one of our horses.

(They ride off.)

Juan Ortiz: I hope De Soto knows what he's doing. I don't trust Tuscaloosa any further than I could throw him.

Francisca Hinestrosa: That wouldn't be very far. He's a huge man.

Juan Ortiz: Exactly. I think we're walking into a trap.

Francisca Hinestrosa: We've already lost almost a hundred men since we landed here. I hate to think how many more we may lose.

Juan Ortiz: You've saved a fair share of lives, Francisca. It's a good thing you were discovered, and De Soto made you a nurse. I confess, though, I don't know why you wanted to come along in the first place. It's too dangerous for a woman.

Francisca Hinestrosa: Anyone who signed up for the expedition knew the risks. I'm in no more danger than anyone else. Besides, what I've seen so far more than makes up for the hard times.

Scene 2: A few days later. In Mauvila (now Mobile, Alabama) outside a Muskhogean village.

Narrator: Chief Tuscaloosa and some of his men accompanied the Spaniards to the village of Mauvila. Hundreds of warriors had gathered inside the village. They were ready to attack. With 200 of his soldiers, De Soto entered Mauvila. The rest of the expedition waited outside the village gates on a plain. All of a sudden, during a festive dinner, the battle erupted. De Soto and most of his soldiers were able to battle their way out of Mauvila. Unfortunately, 13 Spaniards were trapped inside the village. Their fellow Spaniards attacked again and again and finally freed them.

Luis de Mosco: It's a miracle that we got our men out of that village. Another five minutes, and the Indians would have gotten to them.

Hernando De Soto: It's not such a miracle. Look around. Francisca, how many men have we lost?

Francisca Hinestrosa: About 30. Over 200 have been hurt—including yourself, sir. You must let me take care of that wound in your leg.

Hernando De Soto: Almost all of our supplies are gone. They've taken the pearls that Cofita gave us. There *must* be gold in this land. Why else would they fight so hard to keep us out of it?

Francisca Hinestrosa: We must rest here for a while. With that wound, you shouldn't be riding your horse, sir. Many of your men aren't well enough to travel.

Hernando De Soto: Who put you in charge, Francisca?

Francisca Hinestrosa: You did, sir. You made me a nurse. You must trust my judgment in this.

Hernando De Soto: So I will. Luis, tell the men that we'll rest here for a while. Is that all right with you, Francisca?

Francisca Hinestrosa: Yes, sir. That's exactly what I would have ordered.

ACT 4

Scene: Spring, 1541. Inside a hut in an abandoned Chickasaw village.

Narrator: Later in the fall of 1540, the expedition headed into Chickasaw territory. The Spaniards found an abandoned village filled with supplies and decided to stay there for a while. The chief of the Chickasaw brought presents to the Spaniards, but he wasn't pleased to have them in his land.

Bautista: I must say, I'm getting tired of fighting. Maybe we should have stayed in Seville—

Francisca Hinestrosa: You would have been bored. So would I. We'll settle somewhere soon. You'll see. Before long, we'll build a house with a garden, and you'll be wishing you could explore someplace new.

Bautista: I wouldn't want to go exploring without you. Maybe next time you won't have to dress up as a man first.

Francisca Hinestrosa: I'd do it again if I had to.

(Drums and bells sound outside the hut.)

Bautista: Trouble! I knew it!

Francisca Hinestrosa: I smell smoke!

Juan Ortiz: Alarm! Alarm! The Chickasaw! Arm yourselves! We're under attack!

(Francisca and Bautista rush out of the hut. Bautista pulls out his sword and heads for the fighting. As the battle goes on around her, Francisca begins to tend the wounded Spanish soldiers.)

Francisca Hinestrosa: You'll be fine, Gregorio. Let me bandage your arm.

Gregorio: You shouldn't be out here, *señora*. Go back to your hut. Wait until the fighting's over.

Francisca Hinestrosa: I can't do that. Men are hurt. They need my help now.

Gregorio: Oh, no! De Soto's fallen off his horse! He's wounded! No, wait! He's getting up!

Francisca Hinestrosa: I'll go check on him.

Gregorio: No, *señora*! The fighting's too bad over there! *Señora*!

Narrator: De Soto was fortunate. His saddle hadn't been fastened right. He fell off his horse but only bruised himself. Over 10 soldiers were killed in the battle with the Chickasaw. Francisca Hinestrosa was one of them.

Francisca Hinestrosa
Teaching Guide

*In 1598, over 100 women traveled with their fami-
lies into the American southwest with the expedition
of Don Juan de Oñate. They founded the colony of
New Mexico and settled near what is now Los
Alamos.*

Biography

Little is known about the life of Francisca Hinestrosa.
She was married to Hernando Bautista, a soldier, and
they lived in Seville, Spain. With the help of her hus-
band, Francisca disguised herself in men's clothes and joined the Florida expedition
undertaken by Hernando De Soto. In 1541, during a battle with the Chickasaw,
Francisca Hinestrosa was killed. Accounts of her discovery in De Soto's expedition
differ. Some earlier historians say that it wasn't discovered that Francisca Hinestrosa
was a woman until after her death. One source claims that she couldn't escape the
Chickasaw because she was just about to give birth to a baby; another source states
that during the battle with the Chickasaw, she rushed into a burning hut to retrieve a
stash of pearls and was burned to death. Later historians declare that Francisca
Hinestrosa's true identity was discovered sooner, and De Soto relegated her to the
jobs of cook and nurse.

Take a Closer Look

The World's Great Explorers: Hernando De Soto by Robert Carson (Childrens Press, 1991)
Hernando De Soto and the Explorers of the American South by Sylvia Whitman
(Chelsea House, 1991)
Living Dangerously: American Women Who Risked Their Lives for Adventure by
Doreen Rappaport (HarperCollins, 1991)
Extraordinary Hispanic Americans by Susan Sinnott (Childrens Press, 1991)

Activities

Mapping the Action

Francisca Hinestrosa began her journey in Seville, Spain. It ended somewhere in Chickasaw territory in what is now Alabama. De Soto died of malaria on the banks of the Mississippi River on May 21, 1542; however, the expedition continued on. Guide students in researching the route of De Soto's expedition, and then have them create a story map. They may draw or trace world maps and show the expedition's route. Students should place historical markers at important places, explaining the significance of each with a short paragraph.

Explore Exploring

People explore for many reasons. They hope to find riches, claim territory, convert people to a particular religion, study new places and the living things found there, or map new regions. Make a list of the various reasons your students give to explain an explorer's drive and ambition. Ask them to identify reasons that may have motivated Francisca Hinestrosa, and tell why. Extend your discussion to the kinds of explorations that people might undertake today.

That's Debatable

The story of Francisca Hinestrosa brings up many issues regarding women's roles in society. Divide the class into two groups, and hold a debate which focuses on the following questions: Should Francisca Hinestrosa have joined De Soto's expedition or remained in Spain? Should women soldiers fight in combat?

Soldiers in Disguise

Throughout history, women have disguised themselves as soldiers in order to fight, including Joan of Arc in France, Deborah Sampson Gannett (as Robert Shurtleff) during the American Revolution, and Emma Edmonds (disguised as Frankie Thompson) during the Civil War. Ask students to delve into the lives of one of these women and write a play about her.

Where in the World Would You Go?

Although De Soto had enough money of his own to finance an expedition to Florida, he still asked for and received the support of King Charles. If your students could explore any place in the world, where would they go and why? Direct your students to write proposals to their own imaginary sponsors which describe the places they've chosen, explain why their journeys are important, and tell what kind of support they need (money, supplies, information and so on).

Battlefield Nurses

Francisca Hinestrosa lost her life while taking care of wounded soldiers during battle. Many other women have distinguished themselves as nurses on the battlefield. Florence Nightingale ministered to English soldiers in the Crimean War, and Clara Barton served in the Civil War. Both women helped revolutionize the field of medicine. Ask students to uncover the accomplishments of these two women. They may use their data to design a mock museum exhibit that celebrates the women's accomplishments through texts, quotes, maps, illustrations, and photographs.

Pocahontas
Between Two Worlds
By Mary Pat Champeau

Characters (in order of appearance)
Narrators 1&2
Nantaquaus: Chief Powhatan's son
Chief Powhatan: Leader of the Powhatan Indians
Werowances 1&2: Holy men of Powhatan's village
Pocahontas: Chief Powhatan's daughter
John Smith: Jamestown colonist
Powhatan Warriors 3&4 (nonspeaking roles)
Powhatan Warriors 1&2
John Russell: Jamestown colonist

ACT 1

Scene 1: December 29, 1607. Werowocomoco, an Algonquian village near Jamestown, Virginia.

Narrator 1: At birth, Pocahontas received the name "Matoaka," which means "playful one." She was the favorite daughter of Chief Powhatan, leader of a group of Algonquian Indians who lived in what is now Virginia. In 1607 about twelve years after Pocahontas was born, English settlers established a colony called Jamestown near her home in Werowocomoco.

Narrator 2: The English settlers had chosen a bad location for Jamestown. It was swampy which made farming difficult and made it hard to defend. Chief Powhatan and his people had come in contact with white people before, but none had settled so close to Werowocomoco. The English began to trespass in Algonquian territory and steal their food. One day, John Smith was captured in the nearby forest.

Nantaquaus: Father, the prisoner has asked to trade this copper kettle for food.

Powhatan: He is in no position to trade. He's my captive.

Werowance 1: He's our first captive from the settlement. We have to be careful how we treat him.

Powhatan: I want answers from him. His people live near the river, yet they don't plant crops. They have powerful weapons, yet they don't seem to hunt. They have three big boats, yet they don't fish.

Werowance 2: You can never trust someone you don't understand.

Powhatan: I am the Emperor Powhatan. It's my duty to uphold the laws of my people. This man trespassed on our land. He's a thief. Stealing is a very serious crime, punishable by death. Why should I set him free and trade with him? Other thieves have paid dearly for their crimes. After he tells me what I want to know, he too, will die.

Pocahontas: I claim him, Father.

Werowance 1: What a wise child! This is the perfect solution. You can arrange to have the prisoner punished for his crime, Chief Powhatan. Then, just as it seems he's about to be put to death, Pocahontas can step in and claim his life.

Werowance 2: In the eyes of the prisoner, you'll be both a fierce and a fair chief. Fierce enough to enforce our laws and order punishment; fair enough to respect your daughter's right to save a life.

Nantaquaus: It is the law, Father. The right of claiming a life belongs to every member of our tribe.

Powhatan: Then what? If he's claimed by one of us, we must adopt him into the tribe.

Pocahontas: And why shouldn't we adopt him, Father? Peace is better than war, especially in the winter. We need to spend our time gathering food and firewood. If fighting breaks out, we'll lose men and our time to plant and hunt. Let the mighty Powhatan and his people be the first to live in harmony with the whiteman.

Powhatan: Very well. Bring in the prisoner.

Narrator 1: Four Powhatan warriors lead John Smith to a large stone platform and force him to lie down on it.

Smith: Stop! What are you doing? I've come in peace!

Powhatan: You come to steal from me! You must pay with your life!

Narrator 2: As agreed, Nantaquaus approaches the platform and raises a club over his head. Suddenly, Pocahontas rushes to Smith's side and covers his head with her own. Nantaquaus drops his club.

Smith: You saved my life! You're only a little girl! They were going to kill me, and you saved my life! How can I ever repay you?

Pocahontas: Learn and respect our ways. Teach us about your ways.

Smith (sighing in relief): Is that all? I can do that.

ACT 2

Scene 1: May, 1608. Jamestown colony.

Narrator 1: Early in the year, new settlers and supplies arrived in Jamestown from England. A week later, fire swept through the colony and burned it to the ground. Nearly everything was lost. The settlers grew sick and hungry; many died. Chief Powhatan, hearing about the fire, sent Pocahontas with bushels of food and furs to the colonists as a sign of friendship toward John Smith. It was the first of many trips Pocahontas would make as her father's representative.

Narrator 2: An English captain gave Chief Powhatan a gift of 12 swords. This angered John Smith because he didn't want Powhatan and his people to have more weapons. Chief Powhatan admired the swords and asked for more. John Smith refused. As the settlers had been stealing food, the Powhatans began trying to steal more swords. After a fight over a sword in the forest, the settlers captured seven Powhatans. Pocahontas went to Jamestown to ask for their release.

Pocahontas: Captain Smith, you're holding seven of my brothers in your jail.

Smith: That's because seven of your brothers, as you call them, tried to steal my weapons.

Pocahontas: I ask you to release them.

Smith: Why should I? They're thieves.

Pocahontas: My people considered you a thief once. We showed mercy to you.

Smith: I've never been a thief!

Pocahontas: You don't see things the same way we do. If a stranger comes and builds his house on our land and kills our deer and raids our fields, we consider him to be a thief. Just this once, please excuse my brothers for what they've done.

Smith: I can't. We have hardly any weapons left. As leader of the Jamestown Council, it would be irresponsible of me to let the prisoners go. They'll only return later to steal the few swords we have left. I'm down to a hundred men, and most of them are sick. No. I can't risk losing any of my men to sword-stealing Indians.

Pocahontas: Let me tell you how things look through my father's eyes. He has saved your colony by sending your people food throughout the winter.

Smith: That's true.

Pocahontas: You told him you were going to go back home as soon as your ships could make the journey, and so far, you show no signs of leaving.

Smith: True again.

Pocahontas: You accept my father's friendship and call him "father," too. He has asked you many times to lay down your weapons when you enter his house. A son never greets his father with a weapon. And yet, you refuse this request.

Smith: That is indeed true.

Pocahontas: He asks you now to free a few of his men. You owe him that much.

Smith: I suppose I do. But tell him that I'm freeing these men out of gratitude to his daughter, who brings compassion and good advice with her bushels of corn.

Pocahontas: All I hope is that when I return to Werowocomoco with my brothers, my father's heart will soften toward you. As it stands right now, his heart grows harder by the day. If nothing happens to change the course of the path we're on, we will all be very sorry very soon.

ACT 3

Scene 1: December, 1608. A temporary village near Werowocomoco.

Narrator 1: The relationship between the Jamestown settlers and the Powhatan people grew worse. Chief Powhatan no longer trusted John Smith and wanted to be rid of him. Smith, however, continued to go to the chief to ask for more food.

Narrator 2: One night, while Smith and his men slept in a hut in the forest, Powhatan and his warriors made plans. Pocahontas was with them. Pretending to sleep, she listened to her father and his warriors speak.

Powhatan: It's a two-hour walk to their hut. I want 30 of you to go. Wait until after midnight and then set out. It will be easier to surprise them if they're asleep.

Powhatan Warrior 1: How many English are there?

Powhatan: Ten, including Smith.

Powhatan Warrior 2: They loaded their boat with our corn this morning.

Powhatan: Enough! My patience has come to an end. Unload the corn, and then sink the boat.

Scene 2: Later that night. In the settlers hut.

Narrator 1: For the first time in her life, Pocahontas went against her father. She slipped silently away from his camp. With a few hours' head start on the Powhatan warriors, she ran as fast as she could to warn John Smith.

Narrator 2: Smith and his men were sitting around their campfire, eating the last of their supper, when Pocahontas appeared. Surprised to see her so late at night and so out of breath, John Smith jumped to his feet.

Smith: Pocahontas!

Pocahontas: I have to speak to you—in private.

Smith: Here, we'll go into the forest a little ways.

(Pocahontas follows Smith about a hundred feet into the forest.)

Smith: What is it? What's wrong?

Pocahontas: You must return to Jamestown immediately. Leave the boat and the corn. My father's made plans to have you and your men killed. His warriors will be here soon, maybe within the hour.

(Smith rushes back to his camp. Pocahontas follows him.)

Smith (shouting): Men! Pack everything! Put out the fire! We're going back to the fort! NOW! (He turns to Pocahontas and offers her a few beads.)

Pocahontas (shaking her head): I don't want them. I warned you because you've become my friend. I don't want to see any more of my people, or yours, hurt or killed.

Smith: These beads are all I have to give you in thanks for saving my life—again. How can I ever thank you?

Pocahontas: Even if we never see each other again, remember that you were once claimed by Pocahontas, daughter of the Great Emperor Powhatan. Regardless of what happens between our people, you will always be my brother and my friend.

Smith: Don't worry. We'll see each other again. I know we will.

Russell: Smith! Come on! We're ready to go!

Pocahontas: Be safe on your journey back to Jamestown.

Smith: And you on yours.

Narrator 1: Pocahontas never did see Smith again in Virginia. He was injured in a gunpowder explosion and returned to England shortly after Pocahontas saved his life for the last time. The colonists told Powhatan that Smith had died. Whatever friendship existed between the Powhatan people and the Jamestown settlers soon disappeared. Tired of war, Pocahontas left her father's home and joined the Potomac people.

Narrator 2: Unfortunately, her own life was anything but peaceful. An English captain, Samuel Argall, had Pocahontas kidnapped. She was held on a farm near Jamestown and schooled in English ways. After marrying John Rolfe, an English tobacco grower, Pocahontas (now called Rebecca) traveled with him and their baby son to England. There, she was reunited with John Smith. At the age of 23, as she prepared to return to Virginia, Pocahontas fell sick and died.

Pocahontas Teaching Guide

"Were you not afraid to come to my father's country? Did you not cause fear in him, and all his people, but me? . . . I will for ever and ever be your countryman."
    —*Pocahontas to John Smith in London, 1617*

"Being a child of twelve or thirteen, Pocahontas' compassionate heart and courage gave me much cause to respect her . . . Had she not prevailed upon her father to feed us miserable sick creatures that winter, we would have starved."
    —*John Smith, in a letter to Queen Anne, 1616*

Biography

Pocahontas was born in or around 1595. She was the favorite daughter of Chief Powhatan who led 30 Algonquian tribes in what is now eastern Virginia. When she was just 12 years old, Pocahontas began acting as a skillful negotiator between her father and the English colonists at Jamestown—John Smith in particular. She is credited with having kept the failing colony stocked with food and supplies throughout the winter of 1608. The relationship between the Powhatans and the Jamestown settlers soured quickly, however, and brutalities were exchanged on both sides. In 1609, after injuring himself in a gunpowder accident, John Smith sailed back to England. The colonists told Chief Powhatan that John Smith had died. The situation between the two groups continued to deteriorate. Pocahontas, mourning the loss of her friend John Smith and seeking more peaceful surroundings, went to live with the Potomac Indians in 1612. A year later, she was kidnapped by Captain Samuel Argall and held for ransom on a farm near Jamestown. Pocahontas remained on the farm for two years. Where she was trained in English ways and given the Christian name of Rebecca. In 1614, Pocahontas married John Rolfe, an English tobacco grower. One year later she gave birth to a son, Thomas. The family sailed to London and was received in the highest circles of society, due largely to the legendary status of Pocahontas, now known as Lady Rebecca. It was in London that Pocahontas first learned that John Smith wasn't dead. They were reunited in 1617 shortly before Pocahontas contracted smallpox and died as she and her family were about to return to Virginia. She is buried at Gravesend, England. A statue has been erected in her honor there.

Take a Closer Look

Pocahontas and Her World by Philip Barbour (Houghton Miffin, 1970)
The Powhatan Tribes by Christian F. Feest (Chelsea House, 1990)
Pocahontas by Catherine Iannone (Chelsea House, 1996)
Drawing America: Pocahontas, Princess of the River Tribes by Elaine Raphael (Scholastic Inc., 1993)
Captain John Smith's History of Virginia by John Smith (Bobbs-Merrill, 1970)

Activities

War of Words

The conflict between the Jamestown colonists and the Powhatans was often a brutal one. History might be very different if disagreements had been solved using words instead of weapons. Organize peace negotiations between the Powhatans and the English settlers. Divide the class into two groups—the Powhatans and the English. Direct each group to discuss its needs and its problems with the other group. Then bring both sides together to debate their differences. What can both groups do to co-exist peacefully—and help each other?

Peacemakers

Pocahontas was only 12 years old when she began resolving conflicts between her father Chief Powhatan and her friend John Smith. Open a discussion about problem solving by asking your students if they've ever helped resolve a conflict between other people. Ask volunteers to share their experiences. Expand the discussion to include conflicts in the world today. What might students do, individually and collectively, to contribute to peaceful solutions to these problems?

Pocahontas, Part Two

The events described in this play took place when Pocahontas was still a young girl. The next ten years were full of unusual and intriguing experiences as well. Have small groups of students write sequels to this play "Between Two Worlds." Each group should focus on a different aspect of Pocahontas' life such as: her kidnapping by Samuel Argall, her training in English ways, her marriage to John Rolfe, her entrance into English society, her reunion with John Smith, or her early death.

Thumbs Up?

Throughout the years, the relationship between Pocahontas and John Smith has been portrayed in different ways. Some historians question whether she really "saved" the English captain's life. Smith himself didn't refer to the incident in the first account of his experiences in Virginia; he inserted it after meeting Pocahontas again in England. Poll your students to see if any of them have seen the recent animated movie *Pocahontas*. Ask them to write a review of the movie. Their reviews should include a comparison of the events as depicted in the play "Between Two Worlds" and in the movie.

The Not-So-New World

Although Europeans called America the "New World," Native American societies had lived in the region for thousands of years. Powhatan's people had called the forests of Virginia home for more than 4,000 years before the first white settlers arrived in America. After students research the Powhatan culture, encourage them to write a narrative about one topic such as food, shelter, clothing, social structure, religious beliefs, family life, or government. Their narratives should describe daily life as well as special ceremonial days.

Stepping Back in Time

One mile from the original site of Jamestown, in Williamsburg, Virginia, is a replica of the Jamestown Settlement which includes people dressed as settlers, life-size ships, the fort, shops, and an active Powhatan village. Ask students to find out everything they can about this living museum. They may use their information to plan a family vacation, or create a diorama of the museum.

Anne Hutchinson

An Outspoken Woman

By Sarah Glasscock

Characters (in order of appearance)

- **Narrator**
- **Anne Hutchinson:** Puritan woman
- **William Hutchinson:** Anne's husband
- **John Winthrop:** Puritan and first governor of Massachusetts Bay Colony
- **John Cotton:** Puritan minister
- **Faith Hutchinson:** Anne and William's daughter
- **Young Women 1&2**
- **Zachariah Symmes:** Puritan minister
- **Governor Dudley:** Second governor of Massachusetts Bay Colony
- **Margaret Winthrop:** Governor Winthrop's wife
- **John Wilson:** Puritan minister in Boston
- **Tithing Man:** Church official who kept people from leaving during service
- **Mary Dyer:** Puritan woman
- **Magistrates and Ministers 1-4** (nonspeaking roles)

ACT 1

Scene 1: April 8, 1630. Southampton, England.

Narrator: In the 1600s, England had an official church—the church of England. Its leader was the King of England. Anyone who disagreed with the teachings of the church was also going against the king. It was dangerous—and illegal—to disagree with the king. The Puritans, however, believed that the Church of England needed to be changed. Some Puritans decided to sail for America and set up a new community where they would be free to worship as they chose.

Anne Hutchinson: Reverend Cotton, your sermons are always so clear. You answer all my questions and put my mind at rest. I think everyone sailing for America will miss your sermons.

William Hutchinson: I'm certainly glad you're staying here in England, Cotton. If not, Anne would have us packed up and ready to the board the *Griffin*, too.

John Winthrop: We'll miss the Reverend Cotton, Mrs. Hutchinson, but we have many good ministers traveling with us. Think of it! A whole community of Puritans! We'll be free to worship as we choose. We'll be free to speak our minds. Reverend Cotton, your life is in danger here because you speak the truth. You would do well to join us.

John Cotton: I wish you and the others the best of luck, Mr. Winthrop. But my place is here, where there's so little freedom and so much fear.

Anne Hutchinson: Our numbers are growing. The king will surely allow the changes we demand in the church.

John Winthrop: Don't be so sure, Mrs. Hutchinson. We say that the Bible is more important than the leaders of the church. The king doesn't want to give up any power.

Anne Hutchinson: Not many men want to give up power. As for women—we have none to give up.

John Winthrop: You carry more power than you imagine, Mrs. Hutchinson. Your words are strong.

Anne Hutchinson: I speak my mind, Mr. Winthrop. As a Puritan, that is only right.

John Winthrop: It's always wise to think before your speak.

William Hutchinson: Set your mind at rest, Mr. Winthrop. A great deal of thought goes into Anne's words. (shaking hands with John Winthrop) Good luck!

(The Hutchinsons leave.)

John Cotton: It's true. Mrs. Hutchinson does think a great deal.

John Winthrop: She would do well to listen a great deal, too.

Scene 2: Summer, 1634. On the deck of the Griffin as it makes another trip to America.

Narrator: From his pulpit, John Cotton continued to demand changes in the Church of England. In 1632, with their lives in danger, the reverend and his wife had to flee to America. After much thought, Anne Hutchinson and her family followed Reverend Cotton to the Massachusetts Bay Colony which John Winthrop and the Puritans had founded in New England. On the trip, Reverend Zachariah Symmes held church services for the passengers.

Anne Hutchinson: Give me your needle, Faith, and I'll thread it for you.

Faith Hutchinson: The ship rolls so, I can't keep my hands still. How much longer do you think we'll be at sea?

Anne Hutchinson: What would you say if I told you we should reach New England in three weeks?

Faith Hutchinson: I'd say that's not soon enough, Mother.

Young Woman 1: Excuse me, Mrs. Hutchinson? I don't mean to disturb you.

Anne Hutchinson: You cause us no disturbance. Please, sit down. How may I help you?

Young Woman 1: I—we . . . well, we couldn't help but notice that you walked out of Reverend Symmes' service this morning.

Young Woman 2: In the middle of his sermon!

Anne Hutchinson: I disagree with his teachings.

Young Woman 2: But he's a minister! Shouldn't he know what he's talking about?

Anne Hutchinson: Yes, he should.

Young Woman 1: I don't really see how you can disagree with him . . .

Faith Hutchinson: You don't know my mother.

Anne Hutchinson: Puritan teachings are very clear. Success in business and wealth are not signs of God's approval. Reverend Symmes seemed to say this morning that having a fine house and property will get you into heaven. But only God chooses those He will save.

Young Woman 2: I pray every day and obey the commandments. I help others—

Young Woman 1: Then it is what is inside you, rather than the things you do or surround yourself with, that earns God's favor?

Anne Hutchinson: Exactly!

(Reverend Zachariah Symmes approaches the group.)

Zachariah Symmes: Mrs. Hutchinson, I trust you are well? I noted that you left in the middle of my sermon.

Anne Hutchinson: I'm quite well, thank you.

Zachariah Symmes: Ah, then you do find the word of God to be wholesome?

Anne Hutchinson: The word of God is indeed wholesome, Reverend, but your words trouble me.

Zachariah Symmes: I beg your pardon? Perhaps if you'd stayed to hear *all* of my sermon—

Anne Hutchinson: I don't think so. Did you not say that doing good deeds is a sign of God's approval? Anyone can do a good deed. What does that prove?

Zachariah Symmes (growing angry): Ministers preach the word of God. Ordinary men do not. Ordinary women definitely do not.

Anne Hutchinson: When we reach Boston, Reverend Symmes, listen to Reverend Cotton. You'll see that there is something beyond the words you preach. I have many things to say to you, but I fear that you cannot bear them now.

(Reverend Symmes stalks off.)

Young Woman 1: You used such strong words with Reverend Symmes . . .

Young Woman 2: Did you see how red his face got? I've never seen him so angry.

Anne Hutchinson: He is a minister. He should preach our beliefs correctly.

ACT 2

Scene 1: Autumn, 1634. Massachusetts Bay Colony. Inside Governor Dudley's house.

Narrator: Reverend Symmes didn't forget—or forgive—Anne Hutchinson. All newcomers to the Massachusetts Bay Colony had to apply to join the Puritan church there. Both Anne and William Hutchinson applied. Each met with the church leaders and answered their questions. William was accepted immediately into the church. Weeks passed, and Anne received no word. Then one day she was called to the governor's house.

Governor Dudley: Thank you for coming, Mrs. Hutchinson. I believe you already know Reverend Cotton, Reverend Symmes, and Reverend Wilson? They have more questions for you.

Anne Hutchinson: I know Reverend Cotton well, and Reverend Wilson less well. Reverend Symmes is no stranger to me.

Zachariah Symmes: Let's begin. Didn't you say you could predict the future when we were on board the *Griffin*?

Anne Hutchinson: I did not. You might as well say that I am a witch.

Zachariah Symmes: I heard you tell your daughter that we would be in New England in three weeks.

Anne Hutchinson: I did say that, but—

Zachariah Symmes: And didn't it come true?

Anne Hutchinson: Yes, we reached Boston Harbor in three weeks—

Zachariah Symmes: Didn't you argue with me on board the ship? Didn't you tell me that what I was preaching was wrong? Tell us all how useless good deeds are.

Anne Hutchinson: Reverend Cotton, I only tried to explain our Puritan beliefs as you explain them so clearly in your sermons.

John Cotton: I have said before, and say again, that ownership of a home and property, doing well in business and doing good deeds, are not signs of God's approval.

Governor Dudley: So Mrs. Hutchinson was repeating your words, Reverend Cotton?

John Cotton: Yes, she was.

Governor Dudley: Then I see no problem. Mrs. Hutchinson, welcome to the church.

Scene 2: 1635. Massachusetts Bay Colony. Inside John and Margaret Winthrop's house.

Narrator: Although she became a church member, Anne Hutchinson still wasn't fully accepted within the Puritan community. Many women met during the week to discuss the ministers' sermons and other religious matters. Anne Hutchinson hadn't gone to any of these meetings because she didn't think the talk was always serious enough. People began to say that she was too proud. To overcome their criticism, Anne Hutchinson started leading her own meetings.

John Winthrop: Where are you going, Margaret?

Margaret Winthrop: Across the street to the Hutchinson's house. It's the Tuesday meeting. I always go, you know that.

John Winthrop: What goes on in those meetings? It seems that more and more people attend each week.

Margaret Winthrop: Anne usually talks about Reverend Cotton's sermons. She answers questions about what he said. He's sometimes hard to understand.

John Winthrop: If they have questions, they would do better to ask Reverend Cotton himself, or another minister.

Margaret Winthrop: But aren't we here in America so we can hold meetings and discuss things? We wouldn't be able to do this in England. We've been holding meetings since we first arrived.

John Winthrop: Not everyone is as outspoken as Mrs. Hutchinson is. She claims to know too much. A woman like that can be very dangerous, putting ideas into people's minds.

Margaret Winthrop: She's able to explain things very clearly to people. If she worries you so, John, then come with me. See for yourself what goes on.

John Winthrop: No, thank you. I don't need Mrs. Hutchinson to explain anything to me.

ACT **3**

Scene 1: Fall, 1636. Inside the Puritan church in Boston.

Narrator: The Massachusetts Bay Colony was now divided. On one side were Anne Hutchinson and her followers, called Antinomians—people who are against law. On the other side were John Winthrop and most of the ministers. The Reverend John Wheelwright, Anne's brother-in-law, arrived in Boston. The Antinomians wanted him to preach alongside John Cotton in the Boston church. John Winthrop voted against Wheelwright. Since everyone had to agree on important church decisions, Anne Hutchinson and her followers lost. They showed their disappointment.

John Wilson: I have a few announcements before I begin my sermon today. Governor Winthrop has asked me to say that the General Court will meet tomorrow afternoon at two o'clock.

(Anne Hutchinson gets up from her seat and goes to the back of the church.)

Anne Hutchinson: Excuse me, sir, but I don't feel well. I must leave.

Tithing Man: You don't look ill to me, Mrs. Hutchinson. Why don't you take a few deep breaths and return to your seat?

Anne Hutchinson: No, sir, I must leave now.

Tithing Man: Very well. You may go out.

(Mary Dyer and other women begin coming to the back of the church, too.)

Mary Dyer: My child is feverish. I must take her home.

Tithing Man: What's going on here? What are you up to?

Mary Dyer: Feel her forehead. See for yourself how hot it is.

Tithing Man: Go on then. Be quick about it.

Young Woman 1: Leave the door open, sir. I must go, too. My little John is colicky. I don't want him to disturb Reverend Wilson's sermon.

Tithing Man: But he's sleeping! He's not—

Young Woman 1: I'm his mother, aren't I? Do you want me to tell Reverend Wilson why little John cried all during his sermon?

Tithing Man: Out with you then. Be quick! Be quick!

Young Woman 2: An emergency, sir. I'm sure I left my broom too close to the fire. My house will surely burn down if I don't leave right now.

Tithing Man: Now, just a minute here!

(John Winthrop hurries to the back of the church.)

John Winthrop: What's going on here? Why are you letting all these women leave?

Tithing Man: They're ill, Governor, or their children are, or they've got to tend to an emergency.

John Winthrop: Anne Hutchinson is behind this, I know she is. Mark my words: This time she's gone too far.

Scene 2: November, 1637. Inside the Newtown Puritan church.

Narrator: In the summer of 1637, 25 Puritan leaders held a synod. They spelled out a list of 82 errors in the way the Puritan community was thinking. Most of the errors pointed to things Anne Hutchinson and her followers said and did. The Antinomians ignored the list. Governor Winthrop and his followers decided that something stronger had to be done. They put Anne Hutchinson on trial.

John Winthrop: Mrs. Hutchinson, you are called here as one of those that have troubled the peace of this colony and the churches here. You are known to be a woman that has a great share in causing this trouble. You've insulted our churches and their ministers. You've continued to hold meetings in your house, even though the synod outlawed them. You must obey the decision of this Court or you'll be banished from the colony.

Anne Hutchinson: I am called here to answer before you, but I hear no things said against me. What have I said or done? I have never harmed my church or community.

John Winthrop: As I said before, the synod outlawed your meetings, yet you continued to hold them. You must not do anything that goes against the authorities of this colony. You must not encourage others to do so.

Anne Hutchinson: If you have a rule for it from God's word, then please show it to me. I have brought my Bible.

John Winthrop: You show me where it says in the Bible that women may hold meetings and preach the word of God. Is Mrs. Hutchinson guilty or innocent? Let me see a show of hands. Guilty? (All the magistrates and ministers raise their hands, including Winthrop.) Innocent? (No one raises a hand.) Mrs. Hutchinson, it has been decided. You are not fit for our society. You are hereby banished from the Massachusetts Bay Colony.

Anne Hutchinson: I have done nothing wrong. I have only spoken out to help my church and community. That is why we as Puritans came here. Have we forgotten that so soon?

Narrator: Anne Hutchinson and her family left the colony and moved to Portsmouth, Rhode Island. William Hutchinson died four years later. The family then went to New York. Sadly, Anne Hutchinson and most of her children were killed in an Indian attack in 1643.

Anne Hutchinson
Teaching Guide

"Anne Hutchinson [was] a woman with a ready wit and bold spirit." —Governor John Winthrop

Biography

Anne Marbury Hutchinson was born in 1591 in Alford, Lincolnshire, England. Her father, a clergyman, was jailed twice for speaking out against the Church of England. In 1612, Anne married William Hutchinson. They had a total of 14 children. The Hutchinsons often traveled to nearby communities to hear different Puritan ministers preach. In Boston, about 24 miles from Alford, they encountered Reverend Cotton. Anne Hutchinson admired Cotton's teachings and the way in which he presented them. He preached the Covenant of Grace, which meant that God decided who He would save. This was in opposition to the Covenant of Good Works, which stated that someone could earn salvation by doing good works and obeying the commandments. The Puritans suffered persecution in England. John Winthrop, a prominent Puritan, decided to found a community in New England called the Massachusetts Bay Colony. Winthrop and his followers left in 1630. John Cotton and his wife fled to America three years later. And in 1634, Anne Hutchinson and her family sailed to the new colony. After dissent on some church leaders' part due to her outspokenness, Anne Hutchinson was accepted into the Puritan church. William prospered as a merchant in the new colony. Anne began holding meetings in her home, interpreting and questioning the ministers' teachings. The number of people at these meetings grew and began to concern John Winthrop and some of the other leaders of the Massachusetts Bay Colony. Hutchinson and her followers were called Antinomians, or people who are against law. To put an end to the split in the Puritan community, a synod was held in August of 1637. A list of 82 errors in thinking was drawn up, most of which were aimed at the Antinomians. True to their name, the group ignored the council's recommendations. In November of 1637, Anne Hutchinson was put on trial for her beliefs. A panel of magistrates and ministers headed by John Winthrop voted to banish her from the colony. After their banishment, the Hutchinson family and some of Anne's followers moved to Aquidneck, Rhode Island, where they founded a new colony. William Hutchinson died four years later. Anne then took her family to New York. In 1643, all but one of the Hutchinsons were killed in an Indian raid. The surviving child, Susannah, was taken captive. Although she was later rescued, Susannah refused to return to the English settlements.

Take a Closer Look

Anne Hutchinson: Fighter for Religious Freedom by Dennis B. Fradin (Enslow Publications, 1990)
Making Thirteen Colonies by Joy Hakim (Oxford University Press, 1993)
They Led the Way: 14 American Women by Johanna Johnston (Scholastic, Inc., 1973)
A Matter of Conscience: The Trial of Anne Hutchinson by Joan Kane Nichols (Steck-Vaughn, 1993)

Activities

Different Voices in the Community
John Winthrop hoped to set up a model community in America where Puritans would be free to worship. As Anne Hutchinson found out, the Massachusetts Bay Colony could be as oppressive as the monarchy in England. What do students think about the decision to banish Anne Hutchinson from the colony? Today, how do we as Americans deal with different voices within our communities? Ask students to present specific examples of opposing voices in their neighborhoods, city or town, state, and nation. Discuss how the two (or more) sides in each example can forge a compromise.

A Price to Pay
Anne Hutchinson's family accepted her banishment as their own. Ask your students how they would have felt if they were part of the Hutchinson family? Would they have encouraged Anne to speak out, or would they have urged her to keep silent? Was being kicked out of the colony too high a price to pay for supporting religious freedom?

Bill of Rights
Freedom of speech and religious freedom are two of the rights guaranteed in the Bill of Rights. Divide your class into small groups. Have each group develop a graphic organizer that explains the meaning of freedom of speech and shows how it affects them on a daily basis.

A Day in Massachusetts Bay Colony
The Massachusetts Bay Colony was founded over 300 years ago. The way people lived has changed considerably since then. Assign the task of finding out what life was like in the colony. Ask students to consider some of these topics: What did people wear? What did they eat? What kinds of games did children play? What holidays did the Puritans honor, and how did they celebrate? Encourage a diversity of presentations, such as writing a diary entry that details a man's, woman's, or child's typical day or, try celebrating a Puritan holiday in class.

From Boston to Boston
Anne Hutchinson has had an impact on maps of the United States. The Hutchinson River and the Hutchinson River Parkway in New York are named after her. Other places in the northeastern United States are named after places in England. Boston, Massachusetts, for instance, was named after the English city from which many settlers came. How many other connections can students find between American and English place names? After consulting a world atlas, students should draw or trace a world map with an Atlantic view and locate and label the place names they discovered.

Another Outspoken Woman
Mary Dyer, a friend of Anne Hutchinson's, voluntarily left the Massachusetts Bay Colony with the Hutchinsons. She later went to England and converted to the Quaker faith. After returning to America, Mary Dyer spoke out about her Quaker beliefs and was hanged in Boston for doing so. Guide students in researching Mary Dyer's life and the Quaker religion. They may use Venn diagrams to compare the Puritan and Quaker religions, and also the lives of Anne Hutchinson and Mary Dyer.

Daughters of Liberty
Spinning for Liberty
By Sarah Glasscock

Characters (in order of appearance)

Narrator

English Visitor

Patsy Blaire: Boston woman

Helen Dixon: Boston woman

Charity Spencer: Providence Daughter of Liberty

Abigail Goode: Providence Daughter of Liberty

India Bradford: Providence Daughter of Liberty

Elizabeth King: North Carolina Daughter of Liberty

Caroline Harris: North Carolina Daughter of Liberty

Maude Epperson: North Carolina Daughter of Liberty

Betsy Warren: Boston Daughter of Liberty

Deborah Manning: Boston Daughter of Liberty

Thomas Boylston: Boston merchant

ACT 1

Scene 1: 1748. Boston Commons.

Narrator: Women in colonial America often met to work and talk together. As they spun, sewed, and knitted, they discussed events in their communities, their colonies, and the mother country, England. Soon, political groups were being formed by women. In 1748, a group of 300 Boston women held a political rally in the Boston Commons. They set up their spinning wheels and spent the day working to protest the English control of trade.

English Visitor: I say! What's going on here? Why are you sitting in the Commons, doing your spinning? Haven't you got homes?

Patsy Blaire: We have. We've got very nice homes filled with furniture made in England out of *our* trees.

Helen Dixon: We read books printed in England. We wear dresses made out of cloth manufactured in England.

English Visitor: You're very lucky. The English factories are the finest in the world, you know.

Patsy Blaire: We think the colonies should build their own factories and produce their own furniture and books and cloth.

Helen Dixon: Why should we send our natural resources to English factories?

English Visitor: English workers would lose their jobs! Then they'd be angry at the king. That wouldn't do—that wouldn't do at all!

Patsy Blaire: We want to create jobs here in the colonies. We want to keep our money and business here.

Helen Dixon: We've come here today to spin our own cloth, to show people that we don't need to depend on England to supply us with the things we need.

English Visitor: Pardon me for saying so, ladies, but the cloth you spin is very . . . rough. Really—wouldn't you rather feel English cloth against your skin?

Patsy Blaire: You ask us to pay too high a price for English silk.

English Visitor: A few shillings a yard! Surely you can afford that?

Helen Dixon: Not until we're free to produce cloth here, or buy it from any country we choose. It's not a matter of money; it's a matter of liberty. Now if you'll excuse me, sir, we have work to do.

ACT 2

Scene 1: 1766. Providence, Rhode Island.

Narrator: In addition to controlling trade in the colonies, England wanted the colonists to pay taxes on certain goods. In 1765, England passed the Stamp Act. Official stamps had to appear on all important documents, newspapers, pamphlets, advertisements—even playing cards. The stamps cost money, and so were a form of tax. The colonists were outraged. Two groups sprang up to fight the unfair tax. One was a women's group called the Daughters of Liberty. One was a men's group called the Sons of Liberty. These groups formed all over the colonies at about the same time, but the first Daughters of Liberty meeting was probably held in 1766 in Providence, Rhode Island.

Charity Spencer: I refuse to buy the stamps. England needs the money to pay for the soldiers it has sent here to the colonies. I don't want the soldiers here. I won't pay a tax to support them.

Abigail Goode: We have no voice in Parliament. We pay taxes, yet we have no one to speak for us in the English government. That's taxation without representation. It's our money—we should have a say in how it's spent.

India Bradford: The Stamp Act is unfair. We all know that. The question is, what are we going to do about it? I agree with Charity. I won't buy the stamps. I say we ignore the Stamp Act.

Abigail Goode: That may not be enough. We should make sure that no one buys the stamps.

Charity Spencer: How?

Abigail Goode: When the stamps arrive from England, send them back—or take them and make sure they're not sold. The Sons of Liberty are planning to meet the ships. I'll be there, too. As a Daughter of Liberty, I'll be there, too!

India Bradford: The British won't like that. Let's not forget: they have troops stationed here. It would be easy for the king to order them to take the stamps back from us.

Abigail Goode: Not if the stamps are destroyed.

India Bradford: This is a big step. It could lead to real trouble between the colonies and England.

Charity Spencer: There's already real trouble between us. We just ask that we be treated fairly by England.

India Bradford: We're agreed then. We'll meet the British ship coming into our harbor and demand the stamps. Pass the word on to other "daughters" and "sons."

ACT 3

Scene 1: October, 1774. Edenton, North Carolina.

Narrator: Thanks to the resistance of the Daughters and Sons of Liberty, the Stamp Act was repealed in 1766. England soon came up with more taxes. In 1767, the Townshend duties put a tax on tea. The Tea Act of 1773 allowed one English company to sell tea cheaply in the colonies. Colonial merchants couldn't sell their tea at such a low price. In Edenton, North Carolina, the Daughters of Liberty held their own "tea party."

Elizabeth King: Are we going to let the British get away with this? First, they tax our tea! Then they say that one company—one company, the East India Company—can sell their tea at a cheap price to us!

Caroline Harris: No! Down with English tea! Boycott English tea! I threw my tea canister out the window this very morning!

Maude Epperson: It would be tea, wouldn't it? I just love my tea. I won't drink that horrid coffee, I just won't.

Elizabeth King: It's English tea you have to give up, Maude, not American tea. We can brew our own tea out of strawberry leaves or sassafras leaves.

Caroline Harris: My mother used to boil currant leaves to make tea.

Maude Epperson (doubtfully): Are you sure that's safe?

Elizabeth King: The committee has worked hard on the declaration. I'd like to read it and then we can vote on it. (reading from piece of paper) "We cannot be indifferent on any occasion that appears to affect the peace and happiness of our country, and it has been necessary for the public good to enter into several particular resolves. We here and now give up the custom of drinking tea, and we promise not to wear any cloth or clothing made in England." All those Daughters of Liberty in favor of this declaration, please raise your hands.

Caroline Harris (looking around): No need to count hands. Everyone's raised hers, including Maude Epperson. All 51 of us agree.

Maude Epperson: I propose that we send the declaration to the Daughters of Liberty in all the colonies so they may pass it around.

Elizabeth King: Does everyone agree? Good! We're all in favor! Anything else?

Maude Epperson: I was thinking about our American tea. We should call it "liberty" tea.

Elizabeth King: All those in favor? (looking around) Liberty tea, it is!

ACT 4

Scene 1: 1774. Griffin's Wharf on Boston Harbor.

Narrator: The Sons of Liberty in Boston held their own "tea party" in 1774. They boarded three English ships loaded with tea and threw the cargo into Boston Harbor. England was angry at the rebellion and closed Boston Harbor. No goods could be sent to the people of Boston. Still, some warehouses were full of coffee and sugar that had arrived before the harbor was closed. A few merchants began charging high prices for these scarce items. One day, about a hundred Daughters of Liberty—some of them wheeling hand carts—paid a call on one of these merchants.

Betsy Warren: Mr. Thomas Boylston! Open up!

Deborah Manning: We've come for some coffee!

Thomas Boylston (locking the door after him as he leaves his warehouse): So many customers this morning! Good morning, ladies! There's plenty of coffee for all. Luckily, I got a shipment before the British closed Boston Harbor. I've had to raise the price some—it's six shillings a pound. That's not bad, really, not bad at all.

Betsy Warren: It's very bad, Mr. Boylston. Hand over your keys, please.

Thomas Boylston: What?! (laughing nervously) Oh, I see, you're joking! Of course, of course. (winking) Let me unlock the door, and you can just help yourselves.

Deborah Manning: We mean business, Mr. Boylston. Hand over your keys, or we'll break in.

Betsy Warren: Six shillings for a pound of coffee! Shame on you, Mr. Boylston! Shame on you!

Thomas Boylston: I'm a merchant, ladies! How do you expect me to feed my family? I didn't attend the tea party! I didn't throw any tea into Boston Harbor! It's not my fault the harbor's closed! Complain to your husbands about the price of my coffee—it's their fault, not mine!

Deborah Manning: You love money, Mr. Boylston. You love it more than you love your family or your country or your freedom.

Thomas Boylston: What gives you the *freedom* to steal my coffee?

Betsy Warren: We would like you to hand over the keys peacefully, Mr. Boylston. But if you will not, then we will take them from you.

Thomas Boylston: I will not hand them over!

(Deborah Manning takes Thomas Boylston by the neck and throws him into her hand cart. A group of women surround the cart.)

Thomas Boylston: All right! All right! There! (He throws the keys on the ground.)

Narrator: Betsy Warren unlocks the warehouse. The women dump Boylston out of the cart and wheel it into the warehouse. Inside, they work quickly and quietly. In a few minutes, they wheel out their carts which are now loaded with coffee. The Daughters of Liberty then march home.

Deborah Manning (handing Mr. Boylston his keys): We will not make you a rich man, Mr. Boylston, not at the expense of our country. Enjoy your morning, sir.

Daughters of Liberty
Teaching Guide

". . . tea I have not drunk since last Christmas, nor bought a new cap or gown since your defeat at Lexington, and what I never did before, have learned to knit, and am now making stockings of American wool . . . know this—that as free, I can die but once . . . . These are the sentiments of all my sister Americans."
—*Mercy Otis Warren in a letter to a British officer*

Background Information

Since the founding of the colonies, American women have been politically active and have organized themselves informally. Neighboring women often met to work together—spinning, sewing, and knitting. As they worked, they discussed current events in their communities and the world at large. The unfairness of English trading practices was a particular concern to the American colonists, because it fostered economic dependence. To protest the imbalance of trade, a group of Boston women formed The Boston Society for the Promoting of Industry and Frugality and held a political rally in the Boston Commons in 1748. Three hundred women set up their spinning wheels and spent the day working. Tensions continued to grow between the colonists and England. The mother country levied a series of taxes on the Americans. The Stamp Act in 1765 declared that all official documents must carry a stamp, which had to be paid for in silver. Feeling that this was a form of taxation without representation, many colonists rebelled. Out of this rebellion, the Daughters of Liberty and the Sons of Liberty were born in 1766. These organizations seemed to form spontaneously throughout the colonies at the same time. Both groups advocated the boycott of British products and the support of American enterprises. Sometimes, they resorted to more radical means: the Sons of Liberty initiated the Boston Tea Party in 1774; the Daughters of Liberty confiscated goods from merchants who inflated their prices after Boston Harbor was blockaded.

Take a Closer Look

The American Revolutionaries: A History in Their Own Words edited by Milton Meltzer (Thomas Y. Crowell, 1987)
Founding Mothers: Women in America in the Revolutionary Era by Linda Grant De Pauw (Houghton Miffin, 1975)
If You Were There in 1776 by Barbara Brenner (Bradbury Press, 1994)
"Revolutionary Tea" and "Clever Mistress Murray" in *From Sea to Shining Sea: A Treasury of American Folklore and Folk Songs* compiled by Amy L. Cohn (Scholastic Inc., 1993)

Activities

What Would You Give Up?

The Daughters of Liberty supported the boycott of tea and cloth produced in England. They urged American colonists to support American businesses and to produce their own products. What would your students give up for a good cause? Ask them to think about some of their favorite beverages, foods, music and other forms of entertainment. What would have to be at stake before students agreed to participate in a boycott—personal freedom, worker safety or wages, danger to the environment?

Rebels With a Cause

To get their point across, the Daughters of Liberty used a variety of means. They wrote declarations and boycotted businesses. Sometimes the group maneuvered around the law, for example, when they emptied Thomas Boylston's warehouse. Discuss the Daughters of Liberty's action with students. Do they agree or disagree with what the women did? What reasons do students give for their opinions?

Boycott Tea!

The following verses written during colonial times express the sentiments of the Daughters of Liberty:

First, then, throw aside your topknots of pride,
Wear none but your own country linen,
Of Economy boast, let your pride be the most,
To show clothes of your own make and spinning.

Throw aside your Bohea and your Green Hyson tea
And all things with a new-fashion duty;
Procure a good store of the choice Labrador
For there'll soon be enough to suit ye;

Have students design posters to illustrate these verses or to advertise other beliefs of the Daughters of Liberty.

In Their Own Words

Many women's voices were heard before and during the American Revolution. Women such as Abigail Adams, Mercy Otis Warren, Phillis Wheatley, and Ann Stockton wrote letters, diaries, plays, essays, and poems about their times. Guide students in finding works written by one of these, or other women speaking out at the time. Encourage them to write their own poems or essays celebrating the importance of the women's writings.

Revolutionary Heroines

The story of Betsy Ross designing and creating the first American flag is just that—a story. She did, however, create banners and flags for regiments of the American army. Other women and girls pulled their weight during the American Revolution as well. Catherine Smith, a gunsmith, and Elizabeth Hager, a blacksmith, produced weapons for the troops. Women known as "Molly Pitchers" accompanied their husbands into battle and often took their fallen spouses' places in combat. Ask students to research these or other women during the American Revolution. They may use their information to set up a Revolutionary Women Hall of Fame in the classroom.

Nancy Ward

Nanyehi, Beloved Woman
By Sarah Glasscock

Characters (in order of appearance)

Narrators 1-3

Nanyehi: Governor of the Cherokee Women's Council (also known as Nancy Ward)

Kingfisher: Nanyehi's husband

Cherokee Warriors 1-4

Creek Warriors 1-4 (nonspeaking roles)

Old Tassel: Cherokee chief

Dragging Canoe: Nanyehi's cousin, and leader of the Chickamaugans (a group of Cherokee)

John Ross: President of the Cherokee National Committee

Major Ridge: Cherokee leader

ACT 1

Scene 1: Mid-1700s. Battle with the Creeks in what is now the southern United States.

Narrator 1: In the 1700s, the Cherokee people lived in the region of the United States that is now Georgia, North and South Carolina, Tennessee, and Virginia. Both women and men were leaders in the Cherokee government. Cherokee and Creek territories were near each other. Hunting parties from the two tribes often encountered each other, and fights would break out. These fights sometimes turned into wars between the Cherokee and the Creek. Nanyehi, a Cherokee woman, accompanied her husband Kingfisher into one of these battles. As a War Woman, she prepared food, carried water and firewood for the warriors, and was in charge of prisoners.

Nanyehi: Kingfisher—did you hear that?

Kingfisher: It sounded like the call of a mockingbird.

Nanyehi: That's what I thought. It *sounded* like a mockingbird. Listen! There it is again!

Kingfisher: It's a Creek signal!

Narrator 1: As Kingfisher grabs his gun, he also gives a hand signal to his warriors to prepare for battle. Nanyehi quickly puts out the campfire and then passes out water pouches to the men. She stores the food behind a fallen tree and guards it. The Cherokee warriors position themselves behind trees. They listen. Suddenly, a band of Creek warriors jumps into the clearing. The battle begins!

Nanyehi: Behind you, Kingfisher!

Kingfisher (turning and wrestling with a Creek warrior): You'll pay for what you did to my brother!

Narrator 1: A shot rings out. Kingfisher falls to the ground, mortally wounded. Nanyehi rushes to her husband's side.

Nanyehi: Kingfisher! Kingfisher! Please, open your eyes! Kingfisher!

Narrator 1: Realizing that her husband is dead. Nanyehi picks up Kingfisher's gun and begins to fire at the Creek warriors.

Cherokee Warrior 1: It's no use! We should retreat!

Cherokee Warrior 2: We can't win without Kingfisher.

Nanyehi: Kingfisher didn't give his life so we could crawl away in defeat. Use your weapons! NOW!

Narrator 1: The Cherokee warriors led by Nanyehi drive the Creeks away.

Cherokee Warrior 3 (to the retreating Creek warriors): Cowards! Stay away from our hunting grounds!

Cherokee Warrior 4: Kingfisher sacrificed his life for a great win.

Nanyehi: I'll prepare him for our journey home.

Cherokee Warrior 1: Your courage saved us, Nanyehi. You stepped in and took Kingfisher's place.

Cherokee Warrior 2: It's true. Your bravery has earned you the title of Beloved Woman.

Cherokee Warrior 3: You'll have a voice in the Chief's Council.

Cherokee Warrior 4: The women will look up to you as their Governor in the Women's Council. Kingfisher would be proud of what you did, just as we are.

Nanyehi: I wanted to protect my people. Any woman would have done what I did.

ACT 2

Scene 1: 1785. Peace Council held in South Carolina.

Narrator 2: During the American Revolution, both the Americans and the English tried to get Native Americans to fight on their side. The Cherokee wanted to stop more American settlers from moving onto their lands. About one-fourth of the Cherokee, led by Dragging Canoe, sided with the English. The rest of the Cherokee wanted to remain neutral. Unfortunately, the Cherokee people lost much of their land and other property in the war. To save what was left, they agreed to sign a peace treaty with the new United States, the Treaty of Hopewell.

Dragging Canoe: Signing a piece of paper will not give us peace! It won't stop the settlers from moving into our land!

Nanyehi: Cousin, you fought the settlers during their war. How many Cherokee lives were lost? How many of our towns were burned? We have less land today than we did when their war started.

Old Tassel: Your own father was a peace chief, Dragging Canoe. Did you learn nothing from him?

Dragging Canoe: Do the Americans have peace chiefs? No! You talk peace, and they talk a different language. You don't understand them. I do.

Nanyehi: We've come here to talk to the Americans. They'll have to give up some things, and so will we.

Dragging Canoe: The talking's already started. How much land do they want us to give up?

Old Tassel: Everything east of the Appalachian Mountains. But they promise that white settlers won't be allowed into our territory.

Dragging Canoe: What about the settlers that are already here? Does the piece of paper say that they must leave? No!

Nanyehi: The Americans have just fought a long, hard war. They won, it's true, but they don't want to do more fighting right now. They're forming a new government. We have a chance to influence them.

Dragging Canoe: The treaty says that the Americans will do all our trading for us. It says that they will tell us what to do.

Nanyehi: Cousin, the Americans are here. There's nothing we can do about that. What we can do is protect ourselves and our people. This treaty will help us do that. Tomorrow, I will meet with the Americans and present them with the wampum belt the Women's Council has made.

Dragging Canoe: And you think the Americans will care? Do you think they'll understand that a wampum belt is a more precious thing than a piece of paper?

Nanyehi: I've explained to the American commissioners that giving them a wampum belt is a sign of agreement with the Cherokee. We need your strength, Cousin. Don't desert us.

ACT 3

Scene 1: 1817. At a meeting in New Echota, capital of the Cherokee Nation.

Narrator 3: After signing the Treaty of Hopewell, many Cherokee became farmers. Their children went to school and learned English. But, until his death in 1792,

Dragging Canoe led his band of Chickamaugans against the white settlers living in Cherokee territory. The Cherokee signed several more treaties with the United States, losing more land, but white settlers continued to pour into their territory. The United States government decided the Cherokee and other Native American societies in the east should move west of the Mississippi. Another treaty was offered to the Cherokee.

John Ross: Nanyehi, what word do you bring us from the Women's Council?

Nanyehi: We're against the treaty. We've given up enough land.

Major Ridge: Andrew Jackson says we owe this land to the American government. He says that the Cherokee who have moved to Arkansas have taken land from his government.

John Rossi: Jackson also says that more of us should move west. He wants all of our land. If we sign this new treaty, he won't stop.

Nanyehi: First the Americans send us plows and tell us we must be farmers. We have become very good farmers. Now, Jackson offers us rifles and bullets, blankets, and kettles or beaver traps if we move west. He wants us to be hunters again. You men may do as you please. You may go to Arkansas and become hunters, but you'll go alone. None of the women will go with you.

Major Ridge: But—

Nanyehi: *None* of the women will go. We've spoken.

Narrator 3: Like Nanyehi, most of the Cherokee people wanted to stay in their homes. Unfortunately, the Cherokee lost more and more of their land.

Narrator 2: When she was over 80 years old, Nanyehi's home and land were taken away from her. She opened an inn in Tennessee. Nanyehi, also known as Nancy Ward, died in 1824.

Narrator 3: The Cherokee fought their removal to Indian Territory in the West. But in 1838, they were forced to go. Because so many people died along the way, their long trip west is called the Trail of Tears.

Nancy Ward Teaching Guide

"Cherokee mothers do not wish to go to an unknown country . . . . We have raised all of you on the land which we now inhabit . . . . We beg of you not to part with any more of our land."
— *Nanyehi's message to the Cherokee council in 1817*

Biography

Nanyehi was probably born in or around the year 1738 close to the present-day city of Knoxville, Tennessee. Her father was of Cherokee and Delaware descent. Her uncle on her mother's side was Chief Attakullakulla, a famous Cherokee Peace Chief. Nanyehi married Kingfisher, a Cherokee. During the war with the Creeks, she followed her husband into battle. When Kingfisher was killed, Nanyehi retrieved his gun and took his place in the fighting. For this, she was named Beloved Woman. The title of Beloved Woman gave Nanyehi voting rights on the Cherokee Chief's Council and made her Governor of the Women's Council. Nanyehi advocated trying to live peacefully with the white settlers who were moving into Cherokee territory. Although she urged neutrality during the American Revolution (and leaned toward the Patriot side), some Cherokee supported the English. After the war, in 1785, Nanyehi helped negotiate a peace treaty with the United States. At some point during this time, she married Brian Ward, a white man and was called Nancy Ward. By 1817, after white settlers had violated many treaties and the U.S. government had formed its policy of relocating the eastern Native Americans to territory west of the Mississippi, Nanyehi argued against giving up the Cherokee homeland. Nanyehi died in or around the year 1824 before the Cherokee were forced into exile on the Trail of Tears. Her headstone reads: "Princess and Prophetess of Tennessee. The Pocahontas of Tennessee and the Constant Friend of the American Pioneer."

Take a Closer Look

Native American Women by Suzanne Clores (Chelsea Juniors, 1995)
Women in American Indian Society by Rayna Green (Chelsea House, 1992)
When Shall They Rest? The Cherokees' Long Struggle with America by Peter Collier (Holt, Rinehart and Winston, 1973)
Mankiller: A Chief and Her People by Wilma Mankiller (St. Martin's Press, 1993)

Activities

That's Diplomatic!

Nanyehi was well-regarded as a peace negotiator for the Cherokee people. Talk about the skills required for a negotiator and why that role is important in society. Do students consider themselves to be good negotiators? What examples can they give?

Homesick

When she was over 80 years old, Nanyehi was forced to leave her village of Chota. The land was no longer considered part of the Cherokee Nation. She opened an inn near what is now Benton, Tennessee. How would your students feel if their homes were taken away from them and they had to move? Would students want to take along items that reminded them of their old home, or would they rather leave everything behind and start fresh in their new homes?

Draw Up a Treaty

The Cherokee signed over 20 treaties with the United States government. To dramatize the realities of treaties, divide the territory of your classroom or your playground area into two different but equal areas. Have half of your students settle in one area, and the other half move into the other area. What things do students discover that they want or need from the opposite side? Each side should draw up a list of demands, and then negotiate with the other side. When a compromise is reached, the two sides should draw up a treaty.

Brave Women

Because of her bravery, Nanyehi was named Beloved Woman and received power within the Cherokee government. Let students cite other brave American women. The women may be famous historical or contemporary figures or someone the students know. Then students may designate titles and honors to bestow. Have them produce publicity packages that include photographs or drawings of the women, examples of their bravery, their titles, and honors.

Other Voices

Mary (or Molly) Brant was a Mohawk woman who lived during the American Revolution. She and her people supported the English during the war. A British Indian agent said that "one word from her [Mary Brant] goes farther with them [the Iroquois] than a thousand from any white man without exception." Have students learn more about the role of women in Iroquois society. As part of their research, direct them to find Iroquois folktales that feature women. They may use aspects of the folktales as a springboard for presenting their information.

The Trail of Tears

In 1838, the Cherokee people were forced to march west to a new home in Oklahoma. Almost a quarter of them died along the way. Consequently, this relocation is known as the Trail of Tears. Ask students to research the Trail of Tears. Encourage them to pay special attention to visual representations and first-hand accounts of the march. Student may use the images and words in juxtaposition with each other when they present their findings to the class.

Elizabeth Blackwell

The Word No Never Stopped Her
By Sarah Glasscock

Characters (in order of appearance)

Dr. Carole Jefferson: Narrator

Elizabeth Blackwell: First woman doctor in the United States

Dr. James Hadley: Dean of Geneva College

Dr. Webster: Professor of anatomy at Geneva College

Male medical students 1-4 (nonspeaking roles)

Madame Charrier: Chief of nurses at La Maternité

Anna Blackwell: Elizabeth's sister, and a well-known journalist

M. Blot: Surgeon at La Maternité

Emily Blackwell: Elizabeth's sister, and a surgeon

Marie Zakrzewska: Doctor

Family Members 1-4

Crowd Members 1-4 (nonspeaking roles)

James Doogan: A former patient of Dr. Elizabeth Blackwell's

Policeman

ACT 1

Scene 1: November, 1847. A classroom at Geneva College in Geneva, New York

Dr. Carole Jefferson: If it weren't for Elizabeth Blackwell, I might not be a doctor today. Her courage made it possible for other women to attend medical school. In the 1840s, when Elizabeth began applying to medical schools, women students were unheard of. Time after time, she was turned down. Then one day, a letter arrived from a small medical college in New York state. All the medical students had voted to accept Elizabeth Blackwell into the school! Classes had already started so she hurried to Geneva College.

Elizabeth Blackwell: I'm eager to begin classes, Dr. Hadley. I've missed two weeks' lessons already. I want to catch up.

Dr. Hadley: Yes, well, I've come to take you to your first class. Before we go . . . (He pauses and then continues.) Miss Blackwell, while I admire your determination, I feel I must explain something to you. You see, the students . . . the students—

Elizabeth Blackwell: They all voted to accept me into school here. Have some of the students changed their minds?

Dr. Hadley: No . . . no, that's not it . . . exactly. You see, the students . . . well, I might as well come right out and say it. They voted you in as a joke.

Elizabeth Blackwell: A joke?

Dr. Hadley: It was a nice spring day, and they were . . . and we read them your letter and asked them to vote on your request. They didn't take it seriously, you see. They were kidding. We didn't think you'd actually show up, you see.

Elizabeth Blackwell: Dr. Hadley, you sent me a letter telling me I had been accepted. I've paid you for my schooling. They may have meant it as a joke, but I'm here—and I'm not leaving until I'm a doctor. Will you show me to the classroom, please?

Dr. Hadley: If you'll wait out here, I'll just go in and . . . prepare the class.

Dr. Carole Jefferson: Dr. Hadley opens the door and enters the classroom. Elizabeth paces back and forth. She can hear him talking to the other students, but can't make out his words. Finally, the door opens.

Dr. Hadley: Come in, Miss Blackwell. (She enters the classroom.) Gentleman, may I present our new student, Miss Elizabeth Blackwell.

Dr. Carole Jefferson: The classroom was totally silent. As the other students stared, Elizabeth Blackwell calmly made her way to her seat. The lectures began, and she soon forgot all about the other students. That night in her diary, Elizabeth wrote, "My first happy day!"

Scene 2: A few months later. Same classroom at Geneva College.

Dr. Carole Jefferson: Dr. Webster, who taught anatomy, was one of Elizabeth's favorite teachers. He believed she would make a fine doctor. One evening, Elizabeth received a note from Dr. Webster, asking her not to attend class the next day. An operation was to be done, and some of the teachers felt she shouldn't see it with the other students. Elizabeth sat down and quickly wrote Dr. Webster. The next day she showed up for class.

Elizabeth Blackwell: Did you receive my letter?

Dr. Webster: I certainly did. I'm about to read it to the rest of the students. I shall have them vote on whether or not to admit you to the operation.

Elizabeth Blackwell (joking): There's altogether too much voting done at this school!

Dr. Webster: Miss Blackwell, I believe you're right in what you wrote. A doctor must study and see everything that may befall a body.

Elizabeth Blackwell: I *am* willing to compromise. Instead of my usual place in front of the classroom, I would be willing to sit in back. Perhaps then my presence wouldn't bother some of the students so much.

Dr. Webster: No, Miss Blackwell, if they make the right decision, you'll sit where you always sit. Right in front.

Dr. Carole Jefferson: Dr. Webster went into the classroom. Elizabeth was again left in the hall to pace. She could hear him reading her letter to the students. After a few minutes, Dr. Webster opened the door.

Elizabeth Blackwell: May I come in, Dr. Webster?

Dr. Webster: You may, Miss Blackwell. We are particularly honored to have you with us today.

(As Elizabeth enters the classroom, all the male students rise and begin to clap.)

ACT 2

Scene 1: 1849. Inside La Maternité, a French hospital outside of Paris.

Dr. Carole Jefferson: Elizabeth Blackwell graduated from Geneva College—first in her class. She had decided to become a surgeon. The best place to study surgery was at hospitals in Paris, France. None of the French schools would let her in. Did Elizabeth give up? Absolutely not! She took a job in a Paris hospital as a student nurse. Most of the other students were young French women with little education. Still, Elizabeth knew that she would learn a great deal about surgery by watching the doctors at the hospital. She worked long hours; her jobs included cleaning the hospital, caring for patients, and taking notes as doctors and nurses asked their patients questions.

Madame Charrier: Mademoiselle Blackwell, I am going over the notes you took for your teacher. Mademoiselle Mallet says that she did not say all the things you wrote down.

Elizabeth Blackwell (expecting to be scolded): I added some details I had observed about the patient.

Madame Charrier: Yes! Yes! You did well! You are a very smart woman. We have all noticed this. But why are you here, Mademoiselle Blackwell?

Elizabeth Blackwell: I'm here to learn, Madame. There is no better place to do that than at this hospital.

Madame Charrier: True! True! We will make you a fine nurse!

Elizabeth Blackwell: I know you would make me a fine nurse, Madame, but I want to be a surgeon.

Madame Charrier: A surgeon! Oh, mademoiselle, you are too much! I almost believed you!

Scene 2: About six months later. Inside the same hospital.

Dr. Carole Jefferson: Elizabeth got to watch the French doctors perform many difficult operations. The long hours of hard work, however, were beginning to take their toll. She planned to leave the hospital soon, travel for a while and become a surgeon. One night, she was awakened to care for a small baby whose eyes were infected. An accident occurred, and Elizabeth's eyes became infected, too. The infection invaded her entire body, and she became seriously ill. Her sister Anna came to her bedside.

Anna Blackwell: Elizabeth, how are you feeling today? Your forehead doesn't seem as hot as it did yesterday.

Elizabeth Blackwell: I'm feeling much better today. My head doesn't ache. I—Anna! Anna!

Anna Blackwell: What is it? Should I get the doctor?

M. Blot (hurrying in): I'm here. What is it, Elizabeth?

Elizabeth Blackwell: My eyes! I can't see!

M. Blot: It's all right. You have a film over your eyes to protect them. Let me remove it.

Elizabeth Blackwell: There! I can see your face! And Anna, I see you—no! No! It's gone! I can't see!

Dr. Carole Jefferson: Elizabeth lost sight in one eye and damaged the other. A surgeon needs the full use of her eyes. Elizabeth's dreams of becoming a surgeon were gone, but she was still determined to practice medicine.

ACT **3**

Scene 1: 1858. New York Infirmary for Women and Children, New York City.

Dr. Carole Jefferson: After continuing her studies in England, Elizabeth returned to the United States in 1851. She moved to New York City and set up her doctor's office as well as a free clinic for poor families. But, as usual, Dr. Elizabeth Blackwell had bigger ideas. She wanted to open a hospital that would also train women doctors— and she did! In 1858, the New York Infirmary for Women and Children opened its doors. Working with Dr. Elizabeth Blackwell were her younger sister Dr. Emily Blackwell, a surgeon, and Dr. Marie Zakrzewska, who had come to America from Germany to study medicine. Although the hospital was successful, no doctor can make every patient well.

Emily Blackwell: It was a difficult case. You warned the family that she wouldn't get better. You did everything a doctor could do.

Elizabeth Blackwell: I know, but that's not what a family wants to hear. They're taking it very hard. (The sound of people shouting outside can be heard.) Do you hear that?

Marie Zakrzewska (rushing into the room): Come quick! They've blocked the doors and the street! We're trapped!

Emily Blackwell: Who has?

Marie Zakrzewska: The woman who died—her family! They've got shovels and axes!

Elizabeth Blackwell: We must keep calm. Our first duty is to make sure our patients are safe. Emily, you and Marie check on them. I'll go outside and talk to the family.

(Emily and Marie hurry out of the room. Elizabeth goes to the front door and opens it.)

Family Member 1: There she is! Woman doctor! Take that! (He hurls a rock at the door.)

Family Member 2: You killed my cousin! (More rocks hit the door.)

Family Member 3: We'll make sure she doesn't hurt anybody else! Come on! Let's get those patients out of there!

(James Doogan and a policeman make their way to Elizabeth.)

James Doogan (to Elizabeth): There, there, doctor, you'd better make yourself scarce.

Elizabeth Blackwell: No, this is my hospital. This is my problem.

Policeman (shouting): All right, you hooligans! Back off! The paddy wagons'll be here in two minutes, and we'll haul the lot of you off to jail!

Family Member 4: Two minutes is all we need! Just hand her over! We want to practice a little medicine on her!

(The family and mob move toward Elizabeth.)

Policeman (to Elizabeth): You'd better get inside, doctor, or you'll be stitching up your own head.

(Elizabeth reluctantly goes back into the hospital.)

James Doogan: What's your beef with the good doctor here? How many of you has she helped? How many of you has she helped for *free*? Is this the way you thank her?

Family Member 1: She didn't help my sister! She killed her!

James Doogan: And that's a sad thing, to lose someone you love, I know that for a fact. I also know how sick she was. Dr. Blackwell made her last hours comfortable. She sat right beside your sister's bed, didn't she?

Family Member 2: She did. What's that got to do with anything? Doctors aren't supposed to sit! They're supposed to make people get well!

(The family and mob shout in agreement.)

James Doogan: And what did Dr. Blackwell tell you? Did she say that she could cure your sister?

Family Member 3: No . . . but

James Doogan: I didn't think so. She tells the truth. She tells you what you're in for. Am I right? How many of you are alive today because of her? I am. Didn't she help me when I had pneumonia?

Family Member 4 (mumbling): She came in the middle of the night to look after our baby.

Policeman: It's not safe for a woman to be going out at that time of night, but that didn't stop her, did it?

Family Member 4: No. No, it didn't. I guess I'll go home and see my baby.

(The family and mob look at each other, and begin to drift off. Elizabeth opens the front door.)

Police: All's well, Miss—sorry—Dr. Blackwell.

James Doogan: It's a hard road women doctors have.

Elizabeth Blackwell: The more of us there are, the easier it will be. You'll see. Soon people won't think twice about going to a woman doctor.

Scene 2: 1869. New York Infirmary for Women and Children, New York City.

Carole Jefferson: During the Civil War, Elizabeth helped the war effort. She chose women to train as battlefield nurses. The hospital, too, overflowed with people from both sides, Union and Confederate. When the war ended, she turned her sights on bigger ideas. In 1864, the New York State Legislature voted in favor of a women's medical college. Two years later, on April 13, 1866, Dr. Elizabeth Blackwell opened such a college. Fifteen women began the study of medicine. Women could now study medicine in Boston and Philadelphia. But Dr. Elizabeth Blackwell still had work to do.

Emily Blackwell: Can you believe that it's been twenty years since you graduated from Geneva College? You were the *only* woman doctor in America. You aren't alone in your profession anymore!

Elizabeth Blackwell: Still, my work's not done.

Emily Blackwell: Of course not. The school's growing every year, and so is the hospital.

Elizabeth Blackwell: Oh, I think my work here in the United States is done. Europe, though, could use my attention.

Emily Blackwell: Europe! You're not going there? Why? You have everything here in America that you fought so hard for.

Elizabeth Blackwell: That *we* fought so hard for. If I went to England, I know the hospital and school would be in good hands. You're not only a fine surgeon, Emily, you run things here very well.

Emily Blackwell: I know better than to say "No, you can't do that" to you. The English don't know what's about to hit them!

Elizabeth Blackwell
Teaching Guide

"All doubt as to the future, all hesitation as to the rightfulness of my purpose, left me, and never in after-life returned. I knew that, however insignificant my individual effort might be, it was in a right direction."
—From the diary of Elizabeth Blackwell

Biography

Elizabeth Blackwell was born on February 3, 1821, into a progressive English family. Of her eight siblings, a sister Anna was a well-known journalist, a sister Emily became a surgeon, and a brother, Henry, married the suffragist Lucy Stone. The Blackwells were deeply involved in the abolitionist movement. Their father Samuel, owner of a sugar refinery, moved his family to the United States after a fire destroyed his factory. He died a short time later. Elizabeth began her quest to attend medical school in 1844. As the rejections flooded in, she convinced several doctors to teach her privately. Finally, in 1847, a small college in New York state sent an acceptance letter. Elizabeth set out immediately for Geneva Medical School only to learn that her unanimous acceptance by the male students had been a joke. No one expected her to show up. She stood her ground and was allowed to attend classes. Two years later, Elizabeth Blackwell graduated at the head of her class. Determined to become a surgeon, she sailed for Paris, which at the time had the best medical facilities in the world. No French school or doctor would agree to teach a woman. Undeterred, Elizabeth applied to La Maternité, a hospital for women outside of Paris, for training as an apprentice midwife. Despite long hours cleaning the hospital and caring for patients, Elizabeth was able to observe many difficult procedures. One night, she accidentally squirted fluid from an infected baby into her eyes and became seriously ill. The illness caused permanent damage: she lost sight in one eye and damaged the other. Her dreams of becoming a surgeon were dashed. In London, Elizabeth was able to further her medical studies, and in 1851, she returned to the United States to set up practice in New York City. In 1858, Dr. Elizabeth Blackwell, with the help of her sister Dr. Emily Blackwell, opened her own hospital, the New York Infirmary for Women and Children. In 1866, the first medical school for women in New York state was established at the hospital. Dr. Elizabeth Blackwell moved to England and worked successfully to open the field of medicine to women there. She died on May 31, 1910.

Take a Closer Look

The First Woman Doctor by Rachel Baker (Scholastic, 1971)
Elizabeth Blackwell by Jordan Brown (Chelsea House, 1989)
The Life of Elizabeth Blackwell by Elizabeth Schleichert (TFC Books, 1991)

Activities

Never Give Up

People kept saying "no" to Elizabeth Blackwell, but she never gave up her dream of becoming a doctor. If anything, the constant rejection made her more determined than ever. Do your students believe that perseverance and determination can overcome any obstacles? If so, encourage them to provide specific examples. If not, question students about the kinds of obstacles they feel are insurmountable and ask them to give their reasons why. Talk about how the story of Elizabeth Blackwell affected their beliefs.

The First One

When Elizabeth Blackwell began to attend medical school, people stared at her. Children followed her around town. She found it difficult to find a landlord or landlady who would rent a room to her. By the end of the first term, Elizabeth Blackwell had earned the respect of her classmates, teachers, and the Geneva townspeople. Open a discussion about the positive and negative benefits of being the first person to do something. Encourage students who have personal or first-hand knowledge of being the first to do something, to share their stories with the class.

I Want to Be—

Although your students have a few years to decide, ask them what careers appeal to them now. Have them write down the necessary qualifications for their careers in the form of an employment advertisement. If you wish, bring in copies of employment ads from the newspaper for students to study. What qualities do students think their career of choice requires? Which of these qualities do they feel they possess? Draw a template for an employment application on the chalkboard. Include a space for a personal statement where the applicant outlines the unique personal qualities that make her or him perfect for the job. After copying the form on a piece of paper, students should fill it out.

A Job Survey

People are drawn to different jobs for different reasons. Invite students to conduct a survey to find out about people and their work. You may wish to have students work together in groups of three or four to come up with a series of questions to include in their survey. They may survey family members, friends, neighbors, and/or school workers.

Is There a Doctor in the Community?

How many doctors serve your community? How many of them are women? Bring in the yellow pages of the telephone directory for your city or town, or direct students to look up the heading "Physicians" at home to answer the questions. Students may present their data in a bar or circle graph.

Other Firsts for Women

Elizabeth Blackwell was the first woman in America to go to school and become a doctor. Many other American women have been the first to accomplish their goals, too. Begin this activity by asking students to design an award that honors the firsts of American women. Then, have them conduct research to learn more about trailblazing women. On their awards, students should write the women's accomplishments. Each award should be accompanied by a brief biography.

Lucy Stone

Changing Old Ideas
By Kevin Cooke

Characters (in order of appearance)

Narrators 1&2

Lucy Stone: Lecturer for women's rights

Hannah Stone: Lucy's mother

Francis Stone: Lucy's father

Antoinette Brown: Feminist and friend of Lucy Stone's

Miss Adams: Principal of the Female Department at Oberlin College

James Harris: Leader of a mob

Mob Members 1-4

Men 1&2: Speakers at an anti-slavery rally

Stephen Foster: Abolitionist

Henry Blackwell: Lucy Stone's husband

ACT **1** "A woman's lot is hard."

Scene 1: 1837. The Stone family farm at Coy's Hill in Massachusetts.

Narrator 1: Lucy Stone was born August 13, 1818, on her family's farm. Lucy's mother Hannah was sorry to hear she'd had a daughter because she felt a woman's life was so hard. Hannah Stone was right about how hard women's lives were, but her daughter set out to change that.

Lucy Stone: Why should I work as hard a male teacher and get paid half as much? Rhoda only makes one fourth as much as the men. She's been teaching longer than I have, too.

Hannah Stone: Rhoda doesn't have the way you have with your students. You're able to calm down the troublemakers.

Francis Stone: You're up to sixteen dollars a month now. That's good money for a man or a woman. Look what you're doing with it—helping me pay off the money I owe on the farm, putting your brothers through college.

Lucy Stone: I've decided to put myself through college, too.

Francis Stone (laughing): What college would that be? None of 'em take women. What are you going to do—dress up like a boy and sneak in?

Lucy Stone: There's a college in Ohio, Oberlin, that's opened up to women.

Hannah Stone: Ohio? That's so far away. We'll never see you, Lucy.

Francis Stone: And what do you plan on doing once you get your college education? I bet you end up teaching in the same school you teach in right now. Maybe they'll pay you sixteen dollars *and fifty cents* a month. All that money for all that college, and what good will it do?

Hannah Stone: Let her go if she wants it bad enough. A women's life is hard enough.

Francis Stone: A woman's life is hard? I'll trade with you any day. You just let me know when you're ready, Hannah Stone, and I'll do it.

Lucy Stone: I wish you could. You'd see how right mother is.

Francis Stone: How you talk now! What's college going to do to you?

ACT **2** *"They think I am honest, but say they are sorry I believe as I do."*

Scene 1: August, 1847. Oberlin College in Ohio.

Narrator 2: Lucy continued to teach. She sent money home to her father and set some aside for her own education. Oberlin College required an entrance exam, so Lucy also enrolled in several local schools to prepare herself. During this time, two of her sisters fell ill and died. Lucy returned to the farm to help her family. Finally, in 1843, at the age of 24, Lucy entered Oberlin. Only men were allowed to join debating societies at the college, so she started a debating society for women. Word of Lucy's speaking skills soon spread. In 1847, at the age of 29, Lucy Stone graduated.

Antoinette Brown: I guess I can tell you now.

Lucy Stone: Tell me what?

Antoinette Brown: I was warned against you when I first came out to Oberlin. One of the trustees said you were smart, and there was nothing dangerous in your character, but that you had strange and dangerous opinions. He said you supported William Lloyd Garrison's views on abolition, and that you were always talking about women's rights. *And* that you wanted to become a public speaker.

Lucy Stone: It's all true.

Antoinette Brown: The trustee won't be very pleased to see Mr. Garrison at your graduation!

(There's a knock on the door. Lucy opens the door.)

Lucy Stone: Miss Adams! Please come in.

Antoinette Brown: Have they decided? May Lucy read her essay at the graduation exercises?

Miss Adams: I'm afraid they have decided. The faculty doesn't think it would be proper for a woman to be seated with the men students on the stage. They say that Professor Thome must read your essay to the audience, Lucy.

Antoinette Brown: But we've voted. The students picked Lucy to write the graduation essay!

Lucy Stone: What is the point of our writing, if we cannot read to others what we've written?

Miss Adams: Lucy, let Professor Thome read your essay. People will know that you wrote the essay.

Lucy Stone: No. If I can't read my own work at graduation, I certainly won't let him do it. It wouldn't be right. It wouldn't be honest. No.

ACT **3** "The moment that that woman spoke to me she had me at complete command. I would have done anything for her . . . ."

Scene 1: Late 1840s. At an anti-slavery rally in Cape Cod, Massachusetts.

Narrator 1: After graduation, Lucy Stone became a public speaker for the New England Anti-Slavery society. The crowds grew larger at her speeches as more and more people heard about the power of her voice. Feelings were strong on both sides of the slavery issue. There was always the danger of violence. Once, while giving a speech, Lucy was hit in the head by a book someone had thrown at her. Another time, she was pelted with eggs. In Cape Cod, a mob attacked the stage where Lucy Stone and other speakers sat.

James Harris: We've no use for your kind here! We'll not hear one word out of your lying mouths!

Mob Member 1 (grabbing Man 1): What've you got to say now?

Man 1: I'm getting out of here!

Mob Member 2 (grabbing Man 2): What about you?

Man 2: I've got a train to catch?

(The two men run away from the mob. Lucy Stone and Stephen Foster remain on the stage.)

Mob Member 3: Well, if it's not Stephen Foster. You should be home writing songs.

Mob Member 4: It'd be a shame if somebody broke those hands of yours. Guess you couldn't do much writing then.

Stephen Foster: Excuse me, gentlemen, but I'm not going anywhere. I have a speech to give.

(The mob grabs him, tears his coat, and begins to hit him.)

Lucy Stone: You had better run, Stephen!

Stephen Foster: Who'll take care of you?

(Lucy Stone turns to James Harris, the leader of the mob.)

Lucy Stone: I believe this gentleman will. (She takes Harris's arm.) What's your name, sir?

James Harris (reluctantly): Harris, James Harris.

Lucy Stone: Would you ask your friends to let Mr. Foster go?

James Harris: Hey, you two! Hands off the guy!

Mob Member 2: Who says?

James Harris (waving a club): *I* says.

(The mob releases Stephen Foster.)

Lucy Stone: Thank you, Mr. Harris. Now, if you wouldn't mind taking me through this crowd, I'd like to talk to you.

James Harris: Out of the way! Out of the way! Foster, you follow close behind.

Lucy Stone: Do you love your mother, Mr. Harris?

James Harris: Of course I do!

Lucy Stone: And do you have sisters?

James Harris: Two: Jeannie and Katherine.

Lucy Stone: Do you care what happens to them, Mr. Harris? Would you protect them as you're protecting me now?

James Harris: Of course I would!

(Listening, the crowd follows Lucy Stone, James Harris, and Stephen Foster to a tree stump nearby. Stone gets on top of the tree stump to speak.)

Lucy Stone: Right now, south of here, men and women your own ages are being taken from their families. They're being placed on platforms and tree stumps like this one. As their mothers watch, they're being sold to the highest bidder. They will never see their mothers or their fathers or their sisters or brothers again.

Mob Member 1: That's what they're here for!

(James Harris shakes his club at the man. He shuts his mouth.)

Lucy Stone: What gives us the right to say that? Who gives us power over another man, another woman? If a black woman suffers a cut, does she not bleed? Her blood is the same color as mine. When you go home tonight, look at your wife, your mother. I ask you to think about this: How would you feel if they were taken from you tomorrow, and there was nothing you could do about it?

(Moved by Lucy Stone's words, the crowd is silent for a while.)

Mob Member 2 (taking off his hat): I guess we owe Mr. Foster a new coat. (He puts some money into his hat and passes it around.)

ACT 4 "We believe . . . that marriage should be an equal and permanent partnership . . . ."

Scene 1: 1853. Coy's Hill, Brookfield, Massachusetts.

Narrator 2: Lucy Stone also began speaking out about the rights of women, too. In 1853, she gave a speech before the Massachusetts legislature in support of full civil rights for women. Henry Blackwell, a Cincinnati businessman and abolitionist, was in the audience. He wanted to meet Lucy Stone, and he did. She was painting the farmhouse ceiling when Henry Blackwell knocked on the door.

Lucy Stone (opening the door): Yes?

Henry Blackwell: Miss Stone? Pardon me for interrupting—oh dear, I really *am* interrupting you! You're painting! I'm very good with a paintbrush myself. Have you got any old clothes around I could put on? I could have that ceiling finished in no time—

Lucy Stone: Who *are* you?

Henry Blackwell: Oh, of course, you don't know me, 'though I feel I know you. I saw—*heard*—you speak in Massachusetts. I'm Henry Blackwell of Cincinnati. I've brought a letter from William Lloyd Garrison—(searching his pockets) introducing me. It's here somewhere.

Lucy Stone: Are you related to Doctor Elizabeth Blackwell by any chance?

Henry Blackwell: She's my sister!

Lucy Stone: I admire her very much. Why don't you come in?

Henry Blackwell: Miss Stone, would you marry me?

Lucy Stone: What?

Henry Blackwell: I mean it.

Lucy Stone: Mr. Blackwell, I have many doubts about marriage in general. I have a *great* many doubts about you.

Henry Blackwell: Tell me what they are, and I'll see if I can't smooth some of them out. Start with marriage.

Lucy Stone: I don't believe that women should give up their own names, much less any right to their own property, money, children, and lives because they're married. Women have few rights as it is. When they marry, they must give up almost everything.

Henry Blackwell: Our marriage won't be like that. I like your name just fine. I wouldn't ask you to give up anything at all. You know something about my family. My sister is a doctor, the first woman doctor in this country, or the world. My sister Anna is a journalist in Paris. Emily plans to practice medicine, too. I support my sisters in all they do, and all they want to do.

Lucy Stone: Mr. Blackwell, thank you for your offer to paint and your offer to marry, but I must turn you down on both accounts.

Narrator 1: Lucy Stone and Henry Blackwell were married in 1855. Lucy kept her own name, and they read a "Marriage Protest" at their wedding. It stated that marriage was "an equal and permanent partnership and should be so recognized by law."

Narrator 2: Continuing to speak out for equal rights for women and African Americans, Lucy Stone also founded a weekly newspaper called the *Woman's Journal.* Henry Blackwell helped edit the newspaper. After Lucy Stone's death on October 18, 1893, their daughter Alice took over as editor.

Lucy Stone Teaching Guide

A male student who debated Lucy Stone about the rights of women said "that little blue-eyed girl in the calico gown from Massachusetts got up, and by the time she had talked five minutes, she . . . swept . . . away [my arguments] like chaff before the wind . . . . If ever that girl reaches her fiftieth birthday, American women as well as the women of the world will owe her a debt of gratitude they can never repay."

Biography

Lucy Stone was born on August 13, 1818, to Francis and Harriet Stone. By the age of sixteen, like her older sister, she was teaching school—sometimes to students her own age—and sending the money home to help support Coy's Hill, the family farm outside of Brookfield, Massachusetts, and her brothers' university education. Upon hearing that Oberlin College in Ohio had begun accepting women students—a first—Lucy began saving money for her own education. To study for Oberlin's entrance exam, she attended various local academies while continuing to teach. Family emergencies called her back to Coy's Hill and interrupted her studies. Finally, in 1843, Lucy achieved her goal and became a student at Oberlin. She was 24 years old. Learning that women weren't allowed to join the college debating society, Lucy organized her own group for women and was soon making a name for herself as an orator. Deeply concerned with the abolitionist cause, she decided to become a public speaker for that cause after graduation and was hired by the New England Anti-Slavery Society. Stone began coupling equal rights for women with her anti-slavery message. In 1855, she married Henry Blackwell, who was Elizabeth Blackwell's brother and an abolitionist. They struck the word "obey" from their wedding ceremony and produced a "Marriage Protest" that argued for the equality of women within the bounds of marriage. Lucy Stone kept her own name as well. Numerous splits occurred in the women's suffrage and abolitionist movements. The women were asked to put their fight for the vote on hold to allow male African Americans to receive suffrage. Feminists were also at odds on how to achieve suffrage for themselves. Lucy Stone parted company with Susan B. Anthony and Elizabeth Stanton because of their tactics. In 1870, Lucy Stone co-founded the *Woman's Journal* a publication advocating women's suffrage. Her husband Henry was an editor. Lucy Stone died on October 18, 1893, in Dorchester, Massachusetts. Editorship of the *Woman's Journal* was taken over by her daughter Alice.

Take a Closer Look

Bloomers! by Rhoda Blumberg (Bradbury Press, 1993)

The First Women Who Spoke Out by Nancy Smiler Levinson (Dillon Press, 1983)

Lucy Stone Speaking Out for Equality by Andrea Moore Kerr (Rutgers University Press, 1992)

The Day the Women Got the Vote: A Photo History of the Women's Rights Movement by George Sullivan (Scholastic Inc., 1994)

Activities

No Women Need Apply

Lucy Stone was such a powerful speaker that P.T. Barnum tried to hire her! Do your students believe that gender has anything to do with whether or not someone should pursue a particular career? Are there some jobs that they think women, or men, shouldn't do? If so, what are the jobs and what are their reasons? Ask students to offer examples of women and men they know who may be doing nontraditional work.

What's in a Name?

Lucy Stone retained her own name after marrying Henry Blackwell. Their daughter's name was Alice Stone Blackwell. How do your students feel about the issue of names in a marriage? Should a woman keep her own name, take her husband's last name, or do they think it matters? You may also wish to bring in wedding announcements that appear in your local newspaper for students to read. Some announcements state whether a woman will be keeping her name after marriage.

Changing Ideas

Would Lucy Stone be surprised about how women's roles have changed in the 1990s? Students might be surprised to see how those roles have changed. Have them conduct interviews with three generations of their own families—grandparents, parents, or siblings. Work with students in class to create a questionnaire. The questions should focus on areas such as education, careers, clothing, types of chores done at home, and school and after-school activities. Students may interview both females and males. Compare the responses in class. What generalizations do students make about the changes in women's and men's, roles based on the interviews?

Speech! Speech!

Are there any Lucy Stones in your class? Which of your students love to speak out in class? Organize them into a public speaking bureau. Draw up a list of topics, or let the students initiate their own. Let them prepare brief speeches for or against the topics to present to the rest of the class. Afterward, poll the audience to find out how the speeches affected them.

It's Time for a Vote!

In 1919 with the passage of the Nineteenth Amendment, American women received the right to vote. While their fight for suffrage was long and hard, women aren't the only ones who had to fight for the right to vote. It wasn't until 1870, with the ratification of the 15th amendment, that states were prohibited from denying citizens the right to vote based on their race. Even individuals between the ages of 18 and 21 were once denied the right to vote. Have your students research the people, events, and issues involved in the suffrage movement. Ask them to use their research to make an annotated time line of the movement from the 1800s to today.

Ellen Craft

A Train Ride to Freedom
By Patricia Likens

Characters (in order of appearance)

Narrator
William Craft: Enslaved man and Ellen's husband
Ellen Craft: Enslaved woman
Ticket Agent
Train Conductor 1
William Cray: A white passenger
Captain Sherman: A steamship captain
Mr. Pruett: A slave dealer
Custom Officer
Percy Jackson: A white passenger
Yankee Soldier
Train Conductor 2

ACT 1

Scene 1: November, 1848. Macon, Georgia.

Narrator: Ellen Craft was the daughter of a white man and an African American enslaved woman. Ellen, too, was considered a slave. At the age of 11, she was sent to work at a house in Macon, Georgia. There Ellen met William Craft, an enslaved man who worked in the same house until he was hired out as a cabinetmaker. Several years later, Ellen and William received permission from their owners to marry. Soon, they were planning their escape from slavery.

William Craft: If I didn't know it was you, I wouldn't know it was you.

Ellen Craft (doubtfully): We must be crazy. Who's going to believe that I'm an old, white man? Just because I'm wearing men's clothes and my skin is light doesn't mean I'm going fool anybody. What about my voice? My voice is sure to give me away.

William Craft: You're Mr. Johnson—a sick, old, white man. Just groan a lot and shake your head. Besides, I'll be right there to answer any questions.

Ellen Craft (groaning and shaking her head): How's that?

William Craft: Not bad, not bad. One thing we've got to figure out is what to do when somebody asks you to read or write.

Ellen Craft: I'm pretending to be old and sick, right? What if we put my arm in a sling? You can explain that I can't write because I've hurt my arm. I can pretend that my eyes are bad, too.

William Craft: That ought to take care of it. Now, all we need to do is get permission to leave Macon for a few days at Christmas. Once we do that, I'll buy our tickets. (whistling) Macon, Georgia, to Philadelphia, Pennsylvania. I've never traveled so far in my life.

Ellen Craft: It's a long trip from slavery to freedom. I expect it's the longest trip we'll ever take.

Scene 2: December 21, 1848. Early morning at the Macon, Georgia, train station.

Narrator: Ellen and William were given permission to leave Macon over Christmas. Their escape was underway! Ellen bundled herself in men's clothes that she'd sewn herself. She wrapped a muffler around her face and put her arm in a sling. Ellen Craft, an enslaved African American woman, was now Mr. Johnson, a free white man. At the train station, William walked a few steps behind his "master", Mr. Johnson.

Ellen Craft: Two tickets to Savannah, please, for myself and my servant.

Ticket Agent: Two tickets to Savannah, coming right up! Here you go, sir. You'll be in the first car. Your man will be in the last car with the other blacks.

Ellen Craft: No! You can see that I'm injured, I've hurt my arm. I need to have my servant in the same car with me.

Ticket Agent: Sorry, sir, but you know the rules as well as I do. No slaves in the first cars. You need anything, one of the conductors or porters will be more than happy to help you.

Train Conductor 1: ALL ABOARD!

William Craft: That's all right, Mr. Johnson. The conductor, he'll take good care of you. You'll be fine. I'll find you when we get to the Savannah station. You just wait for me to find you, 'cause I will now.

Narrator: Ellen boards the first car reluctantly, watching as William goes to the last car. She sits in a seat beside the window and stares out of it. Suddenly, Ellen recognizes a familiar face.

Ellen Craft (to herself): Mr. Cray! It can't be! Oh, please, don't let him get on this train.

(Mr. Cray walks into the car and stops beside Ellen's seat.)

Mr. Cray: Excuse me, sir. Is this seat taken?

(Ellen shakes her head and turns her face to the window again.)

Mr. Cray: Fine morning, isn't it? (He pauses.) I said (in a louder voice), it's fine morning, isn't it?

(Ellen coughs.)

Mr. Cray: You're not sick are you, sir? I can't afford to catch anything at Christmas time. Maybe I'll just move a few rows down. You don't mind, do you. Can't take any chances. (He hurries to another seat.)

Ellen Craft (softly to herself): No, sir, can't afford to take any chances.

ACT 2

Scene 1: The next day. Aboard a steamer bound for Charleston, South Carolina.

Narrator: Ellen and William were reunited at the Savannah train station. They spent the night at a hotel in the city: Ellen stayed in a room, while William slept in the quarters set aside for enslaved people traveling with their owners. The next morning, they boarded a steamer headed for Charleston, South Carolina, and were separated again. At dinner, Ellen found herself at a table with the steamer captain and a slave dealer.

Captain Sherman: Your boy seems to be very helpful to you, Mr. Johnson.

Ellen Craft: He is, Captain. I treat William well, and he respects that.

Mr. Pruett: You treat him *well*? Whatever for? He's a slave. He doesn't need respect. All he needs is a little food and water, some clothes on his back, and a short leash. You're a fool to travel north with him. He'll leave you lickety-split once you hit Philadelphia—see if he don't.

Ellen Craft: I trust William. I would never mistreat him. That's why I know he would never leave me. He doesn't have to go north to live a better life.

Mr. Pruett: Tell you what, I'll give you my card. When he runs off on you, you get in touch with me. I'll find him. I'll sell him for you, too, if that's what you want. I could get a good piece of change for him at auction.

Ellen Craft: No matter what happens, William is *not* for sale. He never will be. He'll never be separated from his family. *Never.*

Captain Sherman: Ah, Mr. Johnson, I'm sorry to say that Mr. Pruett's probably right. Once your William sets foot on northern soil, I'm afraid he'll run away. I've seen it happen too many times. It doesn't matter how well or how badly you treat your slaves. They'll run away every time.

Ellen Craft (calming down): Then I'll be sure to keep my eyes on William, Captain.

ACT 3

Scene 1: Christmas Eve, 1848. At the Baltimore, Maryland train station.

Narrator: The Crafts arrived in Charleston, South Carolina, and then journeyed to Baltimore, Maryland, the last southern city on their trip. The next stop would be the northern city of Philadelphia. There they would be free. But a Maryland law almost derailed Ellen and William.

Custom Officer: Look, if you insist on taking a slave north with you, Mr. Johnson, you have to sign and post a bond. It's the law in Maryland. How do I know you're not some white abolitionist, pretending to own this slave here? How do I know you won't set him free the minute you get to Philadelphia?

Ellen Craft: I understand all that, but you can see, sir, that I've injured my hand. I can't use it at all. How can you expect me to sign anything?

Custom Officer: How do I know you're not pretending to have a hurt hand? Sign with your other hand then. Do that, post your one dollar fee, and you're free to go.

Ellen Craft: I have arthritis in my other hand. I can't possibly write with it.

Custom Officer: I guess your slave will be staying right here in Baltimore then. Enjoy your trip, Mr. Johnson.

William Craft: Pardon me, sir, but Mr. Johnson really can't sign the bond. He hasn't been able to use his hands for a month now. That's why I'm traveling with him. He can give you the dollar—

Custom Officer: What's the matter? Don't you want to stay here in Baltimore?

Narrator: Just then, Percy Jackson, a passenger on the same train that Ellen (disguised as Mr. Johnson) and William took from Charleston to Baltimore, walks past. He overhears the argument and walks over.

Percy Jackson: Mr. Johnson? What's the trouble here?

Ellen Craft: This officer says I must sign a bond so William can go north with me, but I can't sign anything because of my hands.

Percy Jackson: Officer, what if I sign for Mr. Johnson? I can vouch for him; we traveled in together on the train from Charleston. He's a decent Southern gentleman, not an abolitionist. He's only bringing William along because he needs medical care. Will that do?

Custom Officer: It's your name, sir. I guess you can sign it to anything you want to.

Ellen Craft: Thank you, Mr. Jackson. You don't know what this means to me.

William Craft: Merry Christmas, Mr. Jackson!

Scene 2: Christmas Eve, 1848. Aboard a train about to leave Baltimore for Philadelphia.

Narrator: Thanks to Mr. Jackson, Ellen and William were able to board the train for Philadelphia. For the last time, William helped Mr. Johnson get settled in the "whites only" car and returned to the car where blacks had to sit. On the way, William ran into a Yankee soldier.

Yankee Soldier: Hold it! What are you doing in this car? It's for whites only.

William Craft: I was helping Mr. Johnson. He's my master. He's been very sick.

(Ellen hears William's voice outside her window. She pulls back the curtains and listens.)

Yankee Soldier: So you say. Get your master. I want to see for myself how sick he's been.

William Craft: He's not going to like being disturbed. I just got him all settled—

Yankee Soldier: Just get him. I want to see you two in the train station office in five minutes.

Ellen Craft (opening the window): What's all the commotion? How's a sick man supposed to get any rest with all this racket going on? William! What are you doing? Get on this train! What it if leaves without you? What will I do then? Who'll take care of me? Stop dawdling and get aboard. (looking at the Yankee soldier) Who are you? Why are you outside my window, yelling?

William Craft: That's Mr. Johnson, officer. Mr. Johnson, my master.

Yankee Officer: Sorry, sir, but I can't let you through to Philadelphia unless you show me a document that says you're ill—

Ellen Craft: Document! Haven't I already paid and signed a bond? Can't you Yankees see? Don't I look like a sick man? What do you need a piece of paper for?

Train Conductor 2 (hurrying up to the train): Mr. Johnson! What's the matter? Do you need a doctor? Are you feeling worse?

Yankee Soldier: Do you know this man?

Train Conductor 2: He came into Baltimore on my train. Mr. Johnson's been pretty sick, but William takes good care of him. Oh! You don't think William's going to jump off this train and run away? He wouldn't leave Mr. Johnson. Would you, William?

William Craft (smiling): No, sir. Nothing could make me leave Mr. Johnson.

Ellen Craft: Thank you, conductor. I'm going to write a letter to the railroad telling them how helpful you've been. (to the officer) Are we free to leave now?

Yankee Soldier: Yes, sir. Sorry about the trouble.

Ellen Craft: No harm done. Would you just make sure that William gets on the train without any more trouble? Thank you, officer.

Narrator: Ellen and William Craft arrived safely in Philadelphia on Christmas Day, 1848. Ellen resumed her real identity, and they both took their place in society as free people.

Ellen Craft Teaching Guide

"I would rather go hungry in England a freewoman, than be a slave for the best man that ever breathed upon the American continent."

—*Ellen Craft*

Biography

The exact date of Ellen Craft's birth is not known, but she was probably born in 1827 in Clinton, Georgia. Her mother Maria was an enslaved woman and her father Major James Smith was a white man who "owned" Maria. At the age of 11, Ellen was given as a wedding present to a young bride living in Macon, Georgia. William Craft, also enslaved, worked for the same family in Macon. Years later, Ellen and William married. They began to talk of escaping to the North and devised a plan. Having been hired out as a cabinetmaker, William was able to save some money for train and steamer tickets. Because Ellen's skin color was fair, the couple decided that she would disguise herself as an old, ailing white man named Mr. Johnson who would be accompanied by his servant William. Despite some close calls, the two reached Philadelphia and got in touch with abolitionists living there. The Crafts then moved to Boston. Ellen worked as a seamstress, and William continued his career as a cabinetmaker. They were active and well-known figures in the anti-slavery movement. In October 1850, agents of their Georgia owners appeared in Boston with arrest warrants for the pair. The new Fugitive Slave Act made the warrants legal. The Crafts escaped to Nova Scotia and made their way to England. In England, they wrote and published an account of their escape entitled *Running a Thousand Miles for Freedom, or the Escape of William and Ellen Craft from Slavery*. With their five children, the Crafts eventually returned to Boston and then Georgia after the Civil War ended. With the help of other abolitionists, Ellen and William opened the Southern Industrial School and Labor Enterprise. African American students combined the study of agriculture with work in the school's fields. After the farm was burned by the Ku Klux Klan, it was re-established in Bryan County, Georgia. Ellen Craft died in Charleston, South Carolina, probably in 1897. William Craft died in 1900.

Take a Closer Look

Two Tickets to Freedom: The True Story of Ellen and William Craft, Fugitive Slaves by Florence B. Freedman (Peter Bedrick Books, 1989)

Many Thousand Gone by Virginia Hamilton (Knopf, 1993)

Our Song, Our Toil: The Story of American Slavery as Told by Slaves edited by Michele Stepto (The Millbrook Press, 1994)

Activities

Different Disguises

In order to gain her and William's freedom, Ellen Craft had to disguise herself in men's clothes. In what other ways do students think that enslaved people had to disguise themselves? Encourage them to consider the situations of enslaved people who were denied an education but found ways to learn to read and write; who planned escapes on the Underground Railroad; and who tried to keep in touch with family members sent to other places.

Wanted: Ellen Craft!

Suppose that Ellen and William's plan had been discovered. Have groups of students write a series of descriptions of Ellen Craft (as herself and as Mr. Johnson) that might appear on wanted posters. Each group member should write a description from the following viewpoints: the Crafts "owners" (Ellen as a woman), the ticket agent in Macon, Mr. Pruett on the steamer, Percy Jackson, and the Yankee soldier. If students wish, they may include drawings of Ellen Craft and/or Mr. Johnson with their descriptions.

In Their Own Words

Ellen and William Craft wrote their autobiography which detailed their escape to the North. The lives of many enslaved and formerly enslaved African Americans have been chronicled. Encourage all your students to find narratives by African Americans who endured slavery. Conduct a reading of these works, and invite other classes to attend.

A "Well-Crafted" Story

The Crafts' journey didn't end when they reached the North. To escape arrest under the Fugitive Slave Law, they had to flee to England. Assign a story-map project to pairs of students. Let them draw or trace maps showing both the United States and England. They should number the locations on the map that show Ellen's trip, beginning with her birthplace Clinton, Georgia, and ending in Charleston, South Carolina, where she died. Each location should be accompanied by a short paragraph explaining its significance in Ellen Craft's life.

Home Sweet Home

After their return from England, Ellen and William Craft eventually settled in Georgia. Ask your students if they find it surprising that Ellen and William moved their family back to the South instead of staying in the North? Ask students to talk about the factors that might have prompted their decision.

The Underground Railroad

Many enslaved people in the South escaped to the North by means of the Underground Railroad. This well-traveled route had "conductors" like Harriet Tubman who guided their "passengers" to safety. Ask students to find out more about the workings of the Underground Railroad. To present their information, have them play the part of a free African American newspaper reporter from the North who has assumed the disguise of an enslaved person escaping on the Underground Railroad. They should write a series of newspaper articles describing their journey north.

Ida B. Wells-Barnett
Writing the Wrongs
By Mary Pat Champeau

Characters (in order of appearance)

Narrator

Ray: A grocer

Michael-John: A carpenter

Nelson: A barber

Reverend Porter: A minister

Claude: A farmer

Ida B. Wells: Writer and activist who used the pen name of Iola

Julia Peterson: Memphis woman

Mr. Peterson: Julia's husband, a Memphis shopkeeper

Randolf: Reporter for the *New York Age*

T. Thomas Fortune: Editor of the *New York Age*

ACT 1

Scene 1: Fall, 1889. A black-owned barber shop in Memphis, Tennessee.

Narrator: A group of men is sitting around Nelson's Barber Shop on a warm Memphis afternoon in September. As Reverend Porter gets his hair cut Ray, a neighborhood grocer, is reading aloud an article from a local black newspaper called the *Memphis Free Speech*. The article is written by Iola. Everyone in Memphis knows that it's a pen name—a name made up by the writer—but no one knows who Iola really is.

Ray: Listen to what Iola says in today's *Free Speech*: "Anyone who believes that Negro children are getting the same education as white children has never set foot inside a Negro school."

Michael-John: That Iola's done it again. She gets right down to the heart of the matter and tells it straight out.

Ray: There's more. Listen: "If white schools and Negro schools were really equal, then white students would be spending their days in broken down old school houses without books, desks, paper, ink or chalk."

Nelson: Did you see the article Iola wrote last week? She came right out and said that everybody in town should refuse to sit in the car "reserved" for us on the railroad. It's one thing to say don't board that colored car, here in the shop, between friends, but to write it for all the world to see? She's playing with fire.

Reverend Porter: She's right about our schools, though, whoever she is. I don't know how we can expect our young ones to learn to read and write with no books to read and no paper to write on.

Nelson: Better hold still, Reverend, or I'll clip your ear.

Claude: I can't send my kids to school anyway. I need every pair of hands I can get to work the farm.

Ray: Whoa! Listen to this: "We'd do best to keep our nickels to ourselves. Save your money and get out of Memphis. Move west. Move to a place where your children can get the schooling they need and the future they deserve. Equal education is not going to happen here in Tennessee, not in our lifetime."

Claude: I'll tell you what—Iola's going to get herself killed if she doesn't watch out. She keeps writing stuff like that, one of these days, we're going to find out exactly who this Iola is. We'll be attending her funeral.

Michael-John: She's either brave or stupid, that's for sure.

Reverend Porter: She's not stupid. She sees the truth and writes it—in my book, that makes her about the bravest person in Memphis, or anywhere else.

Ray: She keeps me reading the paper, that's for sure. I get a kick just seeing these kinds of ideas in print.

Act 2

Scene 1: May 26, 1892. At Ida B. Wells' home in Memphis, Tennessee.

Narrator: Ida B. Wells, now half owner of the *Memphis Free Speech*, is packing for a trip to Philadelphia and New York. She intends to visit other African American newspaper editors. She also hopes to begin speaking out in person about the troubles in Memphis.

(There's a knock on the door.)

Ida: Who is it?

Julia: It's me, Ida, Julia Peterson. I need to see you!

Ida (opening the door): What is it, Julia? What are you doing here so late? Don't tell me you came here alone. You know it's not safe.

Julia: I had to come. I just saw tomorrow's edition of the *Free Speech*. You've gone too far this time, Ida. People are beginning to suspect that you're "Iola." I'm really afraid for you. You've got to stop writing these editorials. I mean it.

Ida: What's the point of a newspaper if it's not reporting the news?

Julia: Reporting the news is one thing, but it's something else entirely to stir up trouble with your opinions. (reading from a copy of the *Memphis Free Speech*) "Negro men are being jailed and harmed *not* because they've broken the law but because they are finally starting to make money of their own. They are becoming successful businessmen and the white shopkeepers in Memphis won't stand for it—it's too much competition! We mustn't back down or be afraid. If you have a penny to spend, spend it at a colored man's store. And don't ride the streetcar until you can sit where you want. If the mayor of Memphis won't listen to our voices, then we'll let our money do the talking."

Ida: It's true. You know what's happening in this city. Your own husband's a shopkeeper. Believe me, as soon as somebody notices that he's making a little money, they'll stop him anyway they can.

Julia: I don't care if it's true or not—it's too much. Why do you have to bring the mayor into it? You know better than anyone what can happen to black people who speak their minds.

Ida: I'm a writer. If I don't write what I see—if I don't tell the truth—then my words won't be worth the paper they're printed on.

Julia: There must be another way for you to make your point, a softer way, so people won't get so agitated.

Ida: White people, you mean?

Julia: No, not just white people. There are a lot of black people who are afraid to be seen reading your newspaper.

Ida: Nobody's forcing them to buy it.

Julia (sighing): I can see that I'm not getting anywhere with you. I've come here as a friend, you know that. But mark my words, Ida, no good can come of these articles.

(Suddenly, someone bangs loudly on the door. Both women jump.)

Mr. Peterson: Julia! Are you in there?

Julia: It's James. Oh, he told me not to come over here.

Ida (opening the door): Come in, James, before you break down my door.

Mr. Peterson: Julia, I told you not to come over here.

Julia: I had to. I had to talk to Ida.

Mr. Peterson: It's too dangerous.

Ida: I understand—

Mr. Peterson: So Julia told you about our visitors?

Ida: Visitors?

Mr. Peterson: They wanted to convince me to stop selling the *Free Speech* in my store—or else. I couldn't see their faces, but I recognized some of their voices.

Ida: I do understand, Mr. Peterson. I know how convincing visitors wearing hoods can be.

Mr. Peterson: I've got to look out for Julia and our boys. I'm not saying I won't sell your newspaper, but I'm not going to put it out at the store. Folks who want it can ask me for it. People are watching you, Ida. They're watching all of us. Please, be careful. And please understand why this is the last time we can see you.

Ida: I do understand, but I won't back down. I won't stop writing about the wrongs that are done to us. I have to take my chances.

Julia: Have a safe journey, Ida. It's a good thing you're leaving Memphis for a little while. Maybe things will cool down.

(The Petersons leave.)

Ida: If they think tomorrow's editorial is risky, wait till they see next week's.

ACT 3

Scene 1: May 28, 1892. A luncheonette in Manhattan, New York.

Narrator: Ida is having lunch with T. Thomas Fortune, editor of the newspaper the *New York Age*, when one of his reporters bursts through the door.

Randolf: Here you are! I've got some bad news, Miss Wells, some really bad news.

Ida: What is it?

Fortune: What's happened? Come on, Randolf. Spit it out!

Randolf: It's about the *Memphis Free Speech*

Ida: What is it?

Randolf: It's burned down!

Ida: No! Oh, no! Do you know what happened?

Randolf: A mob. Last night. They attacked the offices, apparently because of one of your editorials. They destroyed everything, and then burned the building right down to the ground.

Fortune: That's unbelievable!

Ida: Was anybody hurt?

Randolf: You will be, if you go back to Memphis. You'll disappear just like those other journalists.

Fortune: That settles it, Ida. You can't go back to Memphis.

Ida: I've been urging people for years to get out of Memphis and find better lives for themselves. Maybe it's time I took my own advice. Maybe it's time to get the message to people everywhere, not just in Memphis.

Fortune: I think I know how you can reach a great number of people. The *New York Age* has a large circulation. I can always use a strong voice on my paper.

Ida: Do you mean it? You're offering me a position on your newspaper?

Randolf: You'd really do that? You'd stay up here in the north? Just like that? I guess I'm a little surprised, Miss Wells. I don't know what I was expecting, but I've just told you that your whole life's work is over—it's gone up in flames—and it hardly seems to bother you.

Ida: It bothers me a great deal, but it doesn't surprise me. It bothers me that we can't stand up for our rights without our businesses and our lives being destroyed. My life's work isn't over, Mr. Randolf, it's just beginning. The real work of fighting for justice still lies ahead. (standing up) Mr. Fortune, I believe I have a deadline to meet. I owe you a story about what happened to a small, truth-speaking newspaper in Memphis, Tennessee, last night.

Narrator: Ida B. Wells never returned to Memphis. She dedicated her life to writing and lecturing on equal rights for all Americans. When women began demanding their right to vote, Ida formed the first black women's suffrage organization and helped lead the famous Women's March on Washington, D.C. in 1913.

She made her home in Chicago, where she married Ferdinand Barnett and raised four children. Ida continued her political activism by forming a powerful league of women's clubs and running for the Illinois State Senate. To this day, Ida B. Wells-Barnett serves as an example of a tireless activist who was never afraid to stand up for what she believed in, regardless of the consequences.

Ida B. Wells-Barnett Teaching Guide

"Any chivalry which depends upon the complexion of the skin can command no honest respect."
—*The Memphis Free Speech, May 21, 1892.*

Biography

Ida B. Wells was born the daughter of slaves in Holly Springs, Mississippi, in 1862. She lost her parents and three of her seven siblings in a yellow fever epidemic when she was sixteen years old. She took a job teaching at a rural school in order to support her surviving brothers and sisters. Ida struck her first blow for civil rights in 1884 when she successfully sued the Chesapeake and Ohio Railroad for discriminating against her on the basis of race. She had been forcibly removed from her seat on the train and instructed to sit in the "colored only" car. Three years later, a higher court overturned the decision. The incident prompted Ida to begin writing a series of impassioned, hard-hitting articles, under the pen name of Iola, for the *Memphis Free Speech*, a local black newspaper. Her editorials attacked Jim Crow laws, inadequate education in black schools, taxes, and literacy tests designed to prevent black men from voting, lynchings, and the unfair treatment of women of all colors. Eventually, Ida became part owner of the newspaper. During this time, she also continued to teach. Infuriated by her frank critiques, however, the Memphis school board fired Ida in 1891, and she devoted herself full-time to activism and writing. After a mob destroyed the newspaper office in 1892, Ida B. Wells relocated to the North. In 1895, she married Ferdinand Lee Barnett, a lawyer and editor of the *Chicago Conservator*. They had four children. Ida B. Wells-Barnett's many accomplishments include being a founding member of the NAACP, organizing the first black women's suffrage movement, and setting up services for victims of the East St. Louis race riots in 1918. At the age of 67, she ran an unsuccessful campaign for the Illinois State Senate. Two years later, in 1931, Ida B. Wells-Barnett died. Her autobiography *Crusade for Justice* was edited by her daughter and published in 1970.

Take a Closer Look

Ida B. Wells and the Antilynching Crusade by Suzanne Freedman (The Millbrook Press, 1994)

Ida B. Wells-Barnett by Steve Klots (Chelsea House, 1995)

The Civil Right Movement In America from 1856 to the Present by Patricia and Frederick McKissack (Childrens Press, 1991)

The Memphis Diary of Ida B. Wells by Ida B. Wells and Miriam Decosta-Williams, ed. (Beacon Press, 1995)

Activities

See It, Say It

Ida B. Wells-Barnett stood up for what she believed in and spoke out against injustice even when it meant putting herself in danger. Spark a discussion among your students about activism with the following questions: Have you ever stood up for something you believed in? What happened? Was your viewpoint a popular one? Do you see anything in the world today which seems unfair? How would you make your opinion known? Do you think that speaking out helps solve problems?

In My Opinion

Newspapers play an important role in democratic societies by giving people the chance to publicize their views and concerns. Bring a variety of newspapers to class, and have students read the letters to the editor and editorials in each one. Afterwards, discuss their responses. With which editorials did they agree and disagree? Why? Which letters did students feel were most effective? Why?

Roving Reporters

As a journalist, Ida B. Wells investigated conditions affecting the lives of African Americans at the turn of the century. Turn students into journalists for a week by asking them to investigate topics in the community which interest them. They should interview people, take pictures (if possible), gather facts, and then write their articles. You may wish to turn your classroom into a newspaper office for a day and produce a class-community newspaper.

Putting Her Stamp on History

In 1990, the United States Post Office honored Ida B. Wells-Barnett by issuing a postage stamp with her likeness on it. No longer in circulation, the stamp is featured in the pamphlet "Celebrating Black History with Stamps" produced by the U.S. Postal Service. Ask students to design a new series of postage stamps commemorating Ida B. Wells-Barnett's accomplishments.

Walk Through History

The history of the struggle for black civil rights in the United States stretches from the days of slavery to the present. Direct students to research this progression and collectively construct an illustrated time line or a mural highlighting key events in the struggle. Each illustration on their time line or mural should be accompanied by a short paragraph explaining the significance of the event.

The Women's Page

For a week, have students keep track of the number of newspaper stories that feature women in a positive light, or that have women's bylines. They may bring in their articles and create a publication called the *Women's Page* for the classroom.

Queen Liliuokalani

Aloha Oe, Farewell to You

By Elmer Luke

Characters (in order of appearance)

Will James: Nine-year-old boy

Ada Sakai: Twelve-year-old girl, Will's cousin

Tour Guide

Queen Liliuokalani (pronounced lee LEE oo oh kah LAH nee):
Last ruler of Hawaii

J.A. Cummins: Appointed member of Hawaiian government

Charles B. Wilson: Advisor to Queen Liliuokalani

Kaipo: Adopted son of Queen Liliuokalani, age 11

Aimoku: Adopted son of Queen Liliuokalani, age 10

Lydia: Adopted daughter of Queen Liliuokalani, age 15

ACT 1

Scene 1: Present day. Iolani Palace on the island of Honolulu.

Will: Wow! What a cool building! What is it?

Ada: This is Iolani Palace. It's the palace of the kings and queens of Hawaii.

Will: Wait a minute. Hawaii's a state. America doesn't have kings and queens.

Ada: Hawaii *used* to be ruled by kings and queens.

Will: Oh. And then they joined the United States, and the kings and queens just became normal people, huh?

Ada: Not exactly. Hawaii became the fiftieth state in 1959. The last ruler, Queen Liliuokalani was overthrown in 1895. This is where she lived.

Tour Guide (walking up to the cousins): Would you like to see more of the palace?

Will: Yeah. I could get really comfortable in a place like this.

Tour Guide: How would you feel about it if you lived here but you weren't allowed to leave? That's what happened to Queen Liliuokalani. She was a prisoner here for eight months.

Will: Why? She was queen, wasn't she? Everybody had to do what she told them to.

Tour Guide: A group of businessmen thought that Queen Liliuokalani should do what *they* wanted her to do.

Scene 2: 1892. Iolani Palace.

Queen Liliuokalani: My people, the Hawaiian people, wish to have a new constitution written.

Charles B. Wilson: You'll run into trouble. The foreign businessmen don't want Hawaiians to have a voice in the government.

Queen Liliuokalani: Those businessmen don't want *me* to have a voice in government, either. They forced the "Bayonet Constitution" on my brother in 1887. No, it's time for a new constitution.

Charles B. Wilson: Wait a while. Think about asking the United States to annex Hawaii. We'd be under their protection then.

Queen Liliuokalani: And their constitution. What would I do, Mr. Wilson? Write songs all day long? I would have to give up my throne if I accepted American protection for my country. There would be no more kings and queens in Hawaii. I'm not ready to do that. What I am ready to do is write a new constitution that gives power back to the Hawaiian people.

Charles B. Wilson: The men who took the power away from your people in the first place are still here. They're even richer and more powerful than they were in 1887.

Queen Liliuokalani: They've gotten that power and wealth at the expense of the Hawaiian people. What does the "Bayonet Constitution" say? A white man may vote in Hawaiian elections. He doesn't have to be a citizen of this country. Hawaiian men whose families have lived here for centuries can vote *only if* they own land and make over six hundred dollars a year. Who owns most of the land now? White men. Who works for these men for low wages? Hawaiian men. No, Mr. Wilson, it's time for a new constitution.

ACT 2

Scene 1: Present day. Iolani Palace.

Tour Guide: Queen Liliuokalani was ready to read the new constitution to her people, but her advisors asked her to wait for a few days. They were afraid that there would be trouble. She agreed. In the meantime, a group of businessmen were plotting to take over the government.

Scene 2: 1893. Iolani Palace.

(The queen's three children burst into the room.)

Kaipo: People say you're not going to be queen anymore!

Aimoku: They say the Americans are going to come onshore and arrest you! You're the queen! They can't do that . . . can they?

Queen Liliuokalani: What amazing stories you've heard! You mustn't believe everything you hear. Kaipo and Aimoku, you look so thirsty and hungry. I know Bernice has made you something special today. She's in the kitchen.

Kaipo and Aimoku: Oh, boy! (They race off.)

Queen Liliuokalani: You too, Lydia. Everything's all right.

Lydia: Tell me the truth, Mother. I've seen the American soldiers on the streets. Who's side are they on? Are they here to help us?

Queen Liliuokalani: All right. Sit down here beside me. A group of businessmen claim they've taken over Hawaii. They've chosen Sanford Dole as their president. Dole and some others are in the government building right now. Mr. Wilson is at the police station, telling them that I won't surrender. The royal troops are still under my control, but I've asked the American government for protection. The businessmen have also asked the American government to help them put down my "revolution." We'll see who the Americans support.

(Wilson comes into the room.)

Charles B. Wilson: I've done everything I can. It's no use. The Americans have said they support Dole and his government. You can call out your troops and start a war, or you can surrender.

Lydia: Surrender! No! What will happen to us?

Queen Liliuokalani (thinking): A war will do too much damage to our country. I'll surrender—under protest—and to the United States government only. Once President Cleveland hears the facts, he'll return me to power.

ACT 3

Scene 1: Present day. Iolani Palace.

Ada: Queen Liliuokalani kept her title as queen, but she didn't have any power at all. She left Iolani Palace and went to live in a house called Washington Place. The businessmen took control of the government. A lot of people were unhappy. Some of them planned to take over the government again and put Liliuokalani back on the throne. One night, a group of these men were caught on the beach with a shipment of guns. Queen Liliuokalani's house was searched. Guns were found in her garden, too. She was arrested and brought back to this room in Iolani Palace.

Scene 2: 1895. Iolani Palace.

Queen Liliuokalani: So you see, I've returned to my palace, my home, at last. I must admit that I wish the circumstances were different. My palace has now become my prison.

Charles B. Wilson: You're charged with trying to overthrow the government. They found guns and ammunition in your garden at Washington Place. You and six others have been sentenced to death. This piece of paper is your—and their—only hope. Sign it, and you'll save seven lives, including your own. Sign it, and all your supporters will be released from jail.

Queen Liliuokalani: What power they've given me! All I have to do is give up my throne and I and others may live "free" lives.

Charles B. Wilson: You can't fight them if you're dead.

Queen Liliuokalani: If it were only my death that I had to worry about, I would not hesitate to meet it. I'll sign the paper. I'll trade my throne for my people's lives.

Scene 3: Present day. Iolani Palace.

Will: So what happened then?

Tour Guide: The government broke their promise to Queen Liliuokalani. The six men were put to death, and the rest of her supporters remained in jail. She was put on trial and sentenced to five years of hard labor and fined $5,000. That sentence wasn't carried out. Queen Liliuokalani was imprisoned in this very room for eight months. She wasn't allowed newspapers or books.

Ada: People could visit her, though, and she spent her time writing songs. One of them was "Aloha Oe."

Farewell to you, farewell to you
O fragrance in the blue depths
One fond embrace and I leave
To meet again.

Farewell to you, farewell to you.

Will: I know that song. I always thought it was a sad song. Now I know why. Queen Liliuokalani was saying good-bye to her country.

Queen Liliuokalani
Teaching Guide

"**I**, *Liliuokalani, by the grace of God and under the constitution of the Hawaiian kingdom Queen, do hereby solemnly protest against any and all acts done against myself and the constitutional government of the Hawaiian kingdom by certain persons claiming to have established a Provisional Government of and for this kingdom . . . . Now, to avoid any collision of armed forces, and perhaps the loss of life, I do, under this protest and impelled by said forces, yield my authority until such time as the Government of the United States shall, upon the facts being presented to it, undo the action of its representative, and reinstate me in the authority which I claim as the constitutional sovereign of the Hawaiian Islands.*"

—*Queen Liliuokalani's protest statement*

Biography

The last reigning monarch of the Hawaiian Islands was born in Honolulu on September 2, 1838. Liliu Kamakaeha was her Hawaiian name, Lydia was her Christian name, and upon the coronation of her brother David Kalakaua as king, she was given the name Liliuokalani. When her brother died in 1891, Liliuokalani became queen. She inherited an unhappy situation of political turmoil and uncertainty. The economics of sugar and the logistics of the islands situated midway between the United States and Asia had brought great American interest to the islands. This interest was in large part represented by descendants of the Protestant missionary families who had arrived in the islands around 1820; they called themselves the Missionary Party or the Reform Party. In time, a Western-style constitutional government, which the Hawaiians had never before known, was imposed upon the monarchy by this increasingly powerful party. King Kalakaua had attempted to promote a native Hawaiian nationalism, but his efforts were crushed when he was forced to sign what became known as the "Bayonet Constitution." By this document, the sovereignty of the monarchy was reduced, and the voting rights of Hawaiians were effectively curtailed. A person now had to own property and earn at least six hundred dollars a year to gain suffrage—although being a citizen of Hawaii was not required. Queen Liliuokalani exercised what power the "Bayonet Constitution" afforded her. She proposed a new constitution that would restore authority to the crown and voting rights to the Hawaiian people. In 1893, the government was seized with the help of American soldiers from the *U.S.S. Boston*. A provisional government headed by Sanford Dole as president was set up. Liliuokalani surrendered under protest. She retained the title of queen but had no power. In 1895, when it appeared that Liliuokalani was leading an insurrection against the provisional government, she was tried for treason and imprisoned in Iolani Palace for eight months. On January 24, 1895, Queen Liliuokalani abdicated the throne. She died on November 11, 1917, in Honolulu.

Take a Closer Look
Hawaii's Story By Hawaii's Queen by Liliuokalani (Charles E. Tuttle Company, 1964)
Liliuokalani: Queen of Hawaii by Mary Malone (Chelsea House, 1993)
The Last Princess: The Story of Princess Ka'ilulani of Hawaii by Fay Stanley
(Four Winds Press, 1991)

Activities

Monarchs and Presidents
Although Hawaii had a constitution, the country was headed by a monarchy. The United States has a constitution, too, but it's led by a president. Ask students to describe the differences between a king or queen and a president. How does each type of leader gain power? Why do students think that women have ruled monarchies for centuries, yet an American woman hasn't yet served as president? Would Queen Liliuokalani have made a good president?

What I Know About Hawaii
Hawaii's tropical climate and spectacular beaches and mountains make it a popular vacation spot. What perceptions about the Hawaiian Islands do your students have? Write the word *Hawaii* on the chalkboard or say the word out loud. Direct students to say the first words that pop into their heads. Make a list of their impressions on the chalkboard. What kind of overall impression does their list produce? Have any of your students visited the Hawaiian Islands? If so, ask them to share their experiences with the class.

Songs of Beauty
Queen Liliuokalani used her time as a prisoner well. She wrote songs during the eight months she was confined to Iolani Palace. Three of the songs were smuggled out to Chicago and published. The beauty of Hawaii is a frequent theme in her music. Let students celebrate the beauty of their own surroundings by writing songs or poems. You may wish to supply copies of Liliuokalani's songs for students to study.

A Classroom Constitution
The United States Constitution guarantees important freedoms to all Americans. The "Bayonet Constitution" instituted in Hawaii by business interests limited freedom for many Hawaiians—ordinary people as well as its kings and queens. What rights do students believe they should enjoy in the classroom? Divide the class into small groups, and direct each group to draft a classroom constitution spelling out their liberties and responsibilities. After each constitution has been read, students may vote on which one to implement.

Glottal Stops and Macrons
Queen Liliuokalani was also instrumental in leading the fight to preserve native Hawaiian culture, including the Hawaiian language. Students may have trouble at first pronouncing

Liliuokalani's name. Every vowel in a Hawaiian word is sounded. There are five vowels and seven consonants in the language. It also makes use of two diacritical marks: the glottal stop and the macron. Ask students to find out more about the Hawaiian language. They may present their research in the form of a language lesson that describes the vowels and consonants and how the diacritical marks are used. Their lessons should also show how to pronounce at least five different Hawaiian words and give their meanings.